BROOKINGS SUNSETS

GOLD

Photographs by Elizabeth Kramer

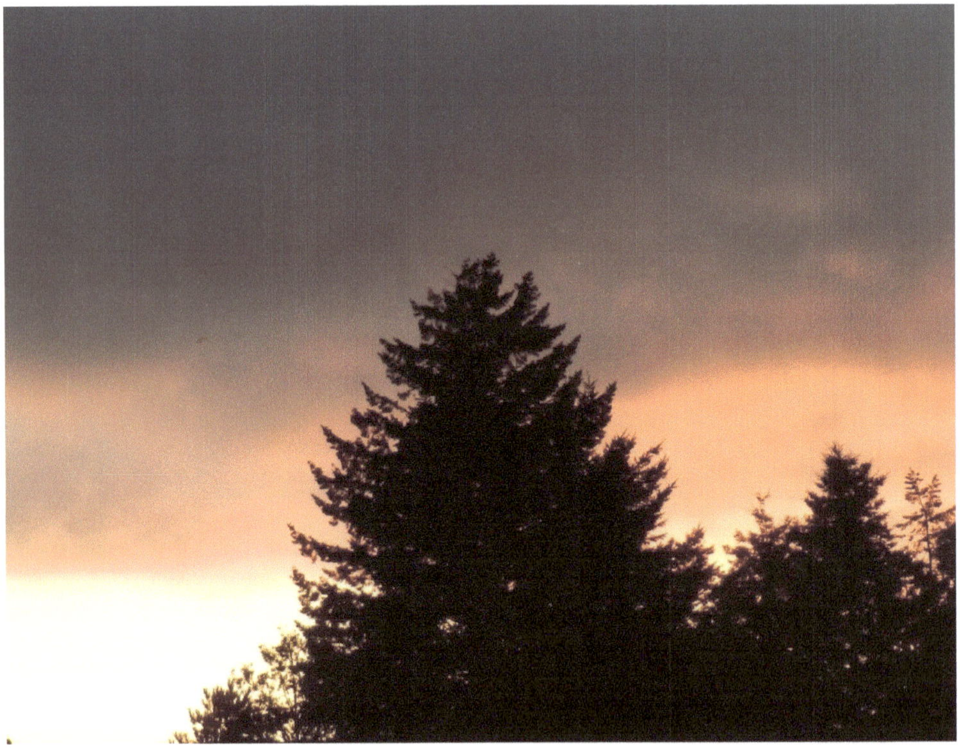

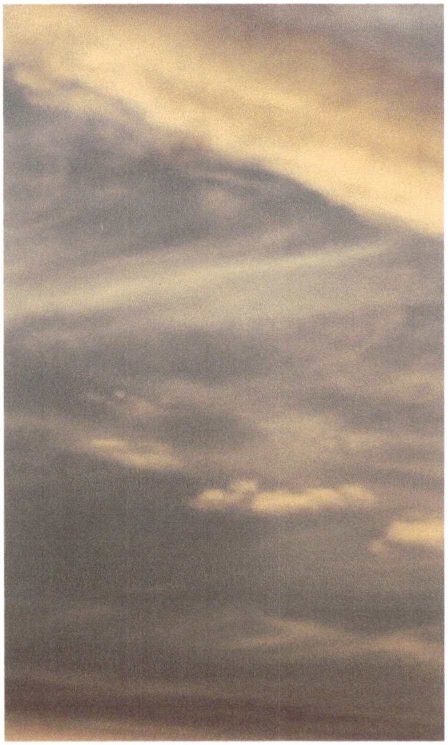

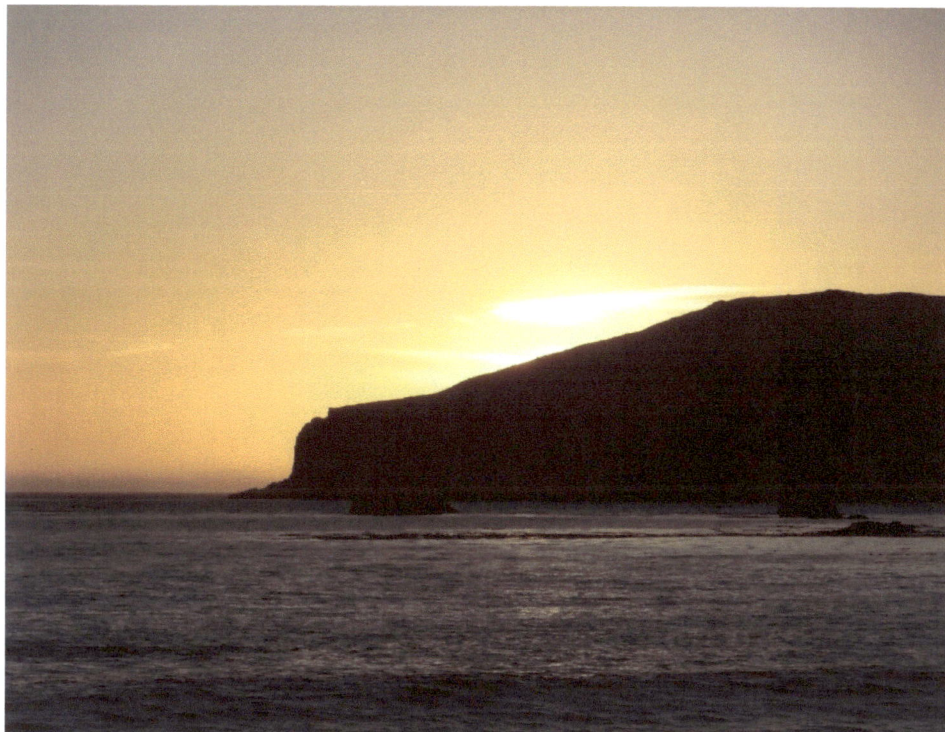

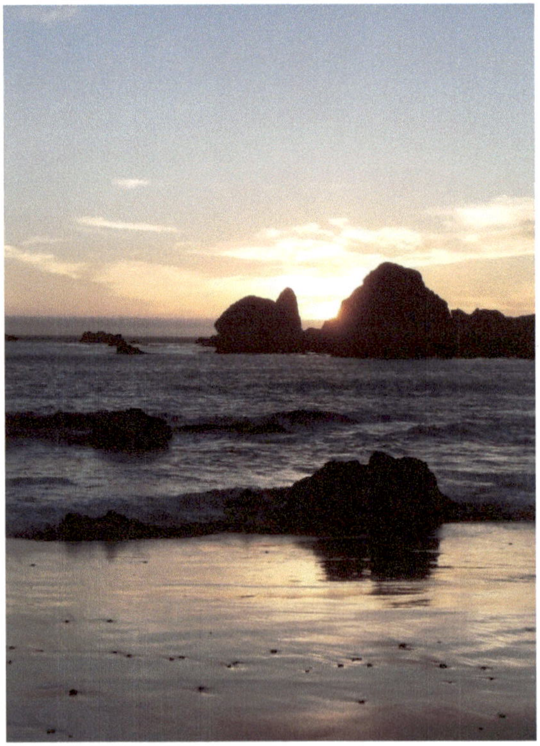

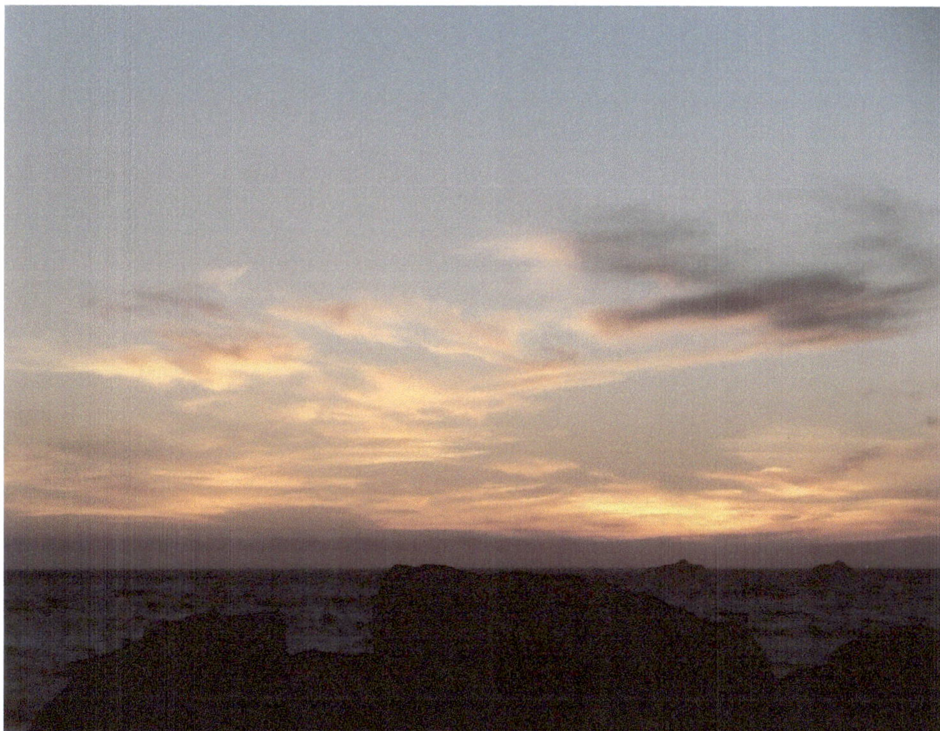

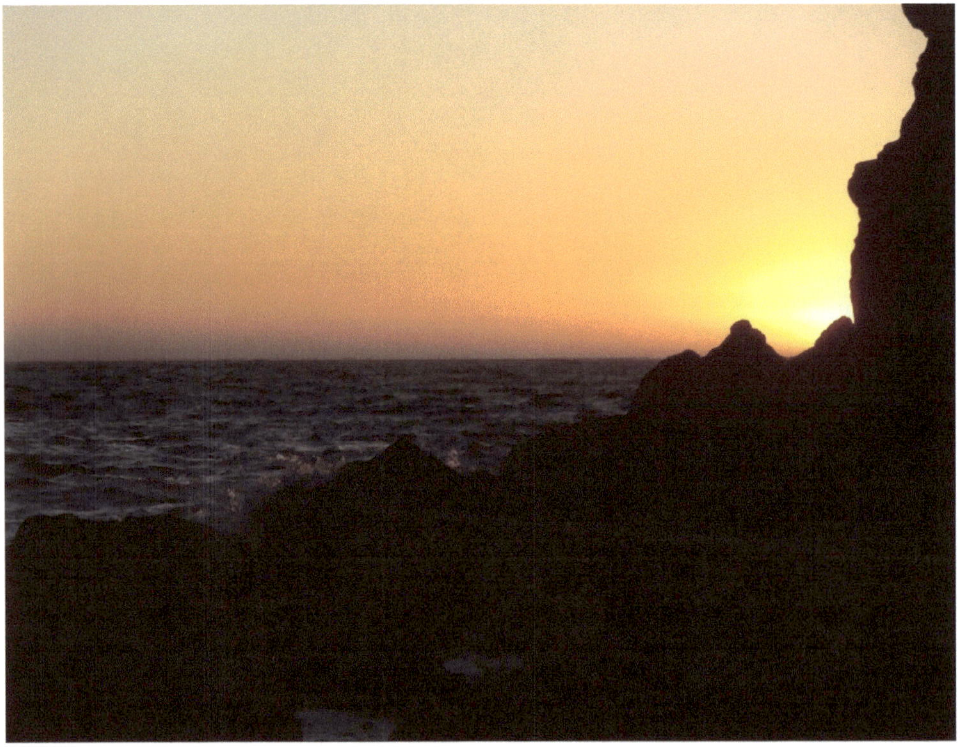

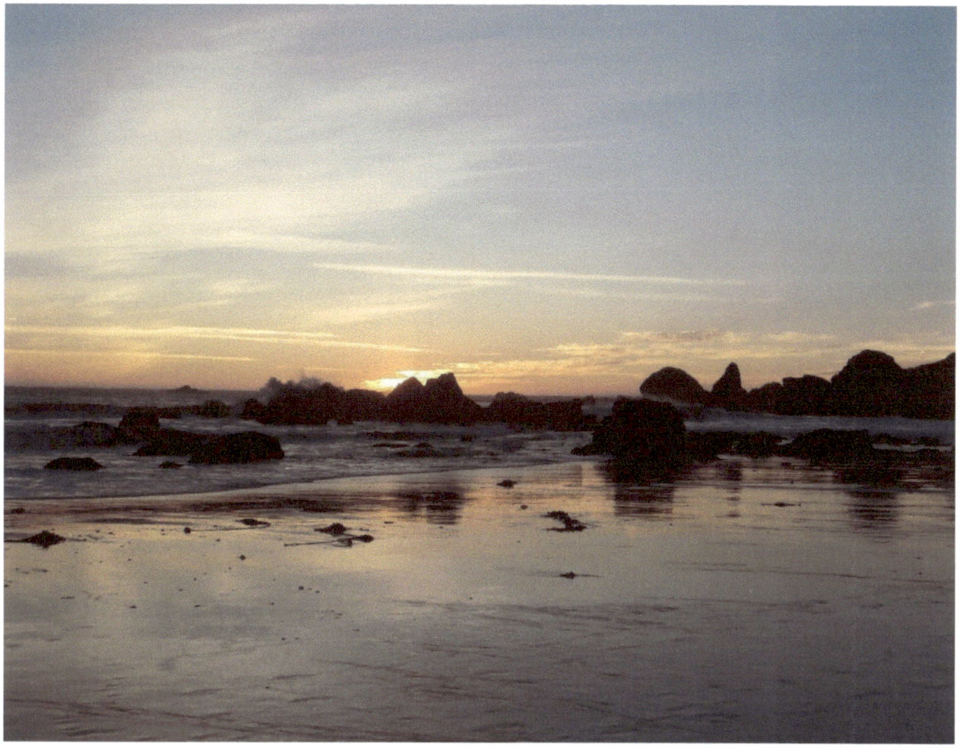

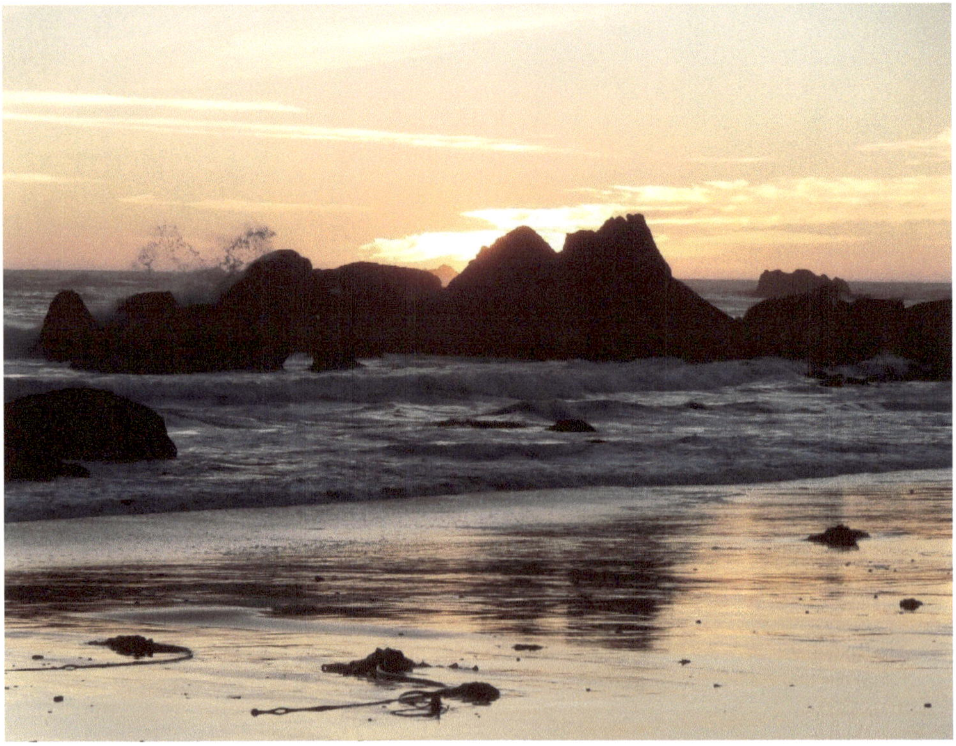

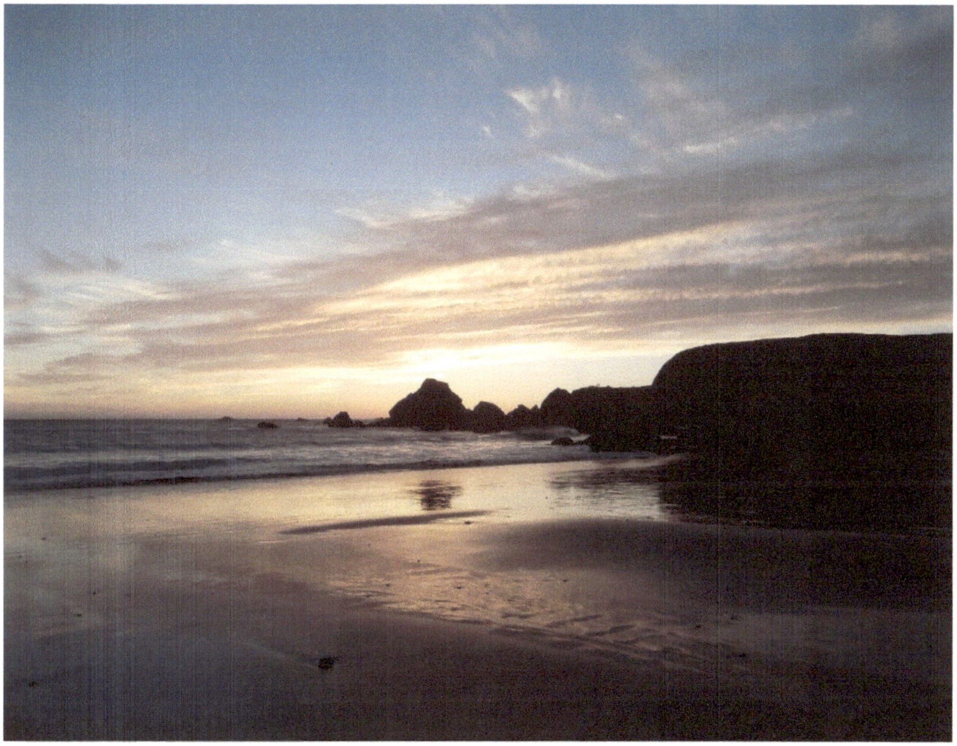

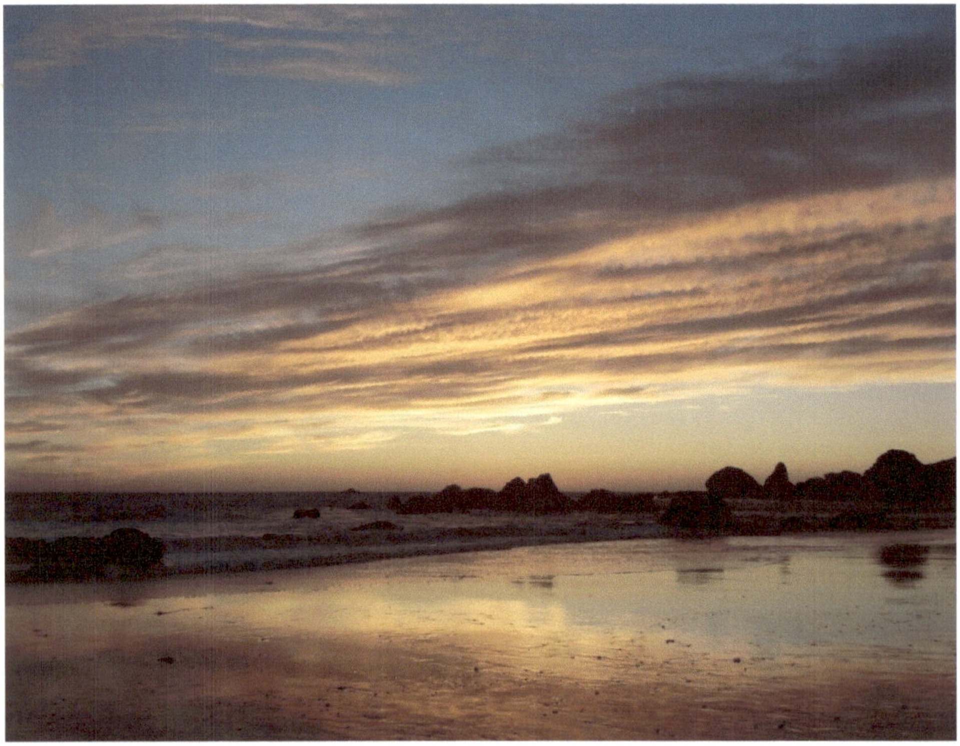

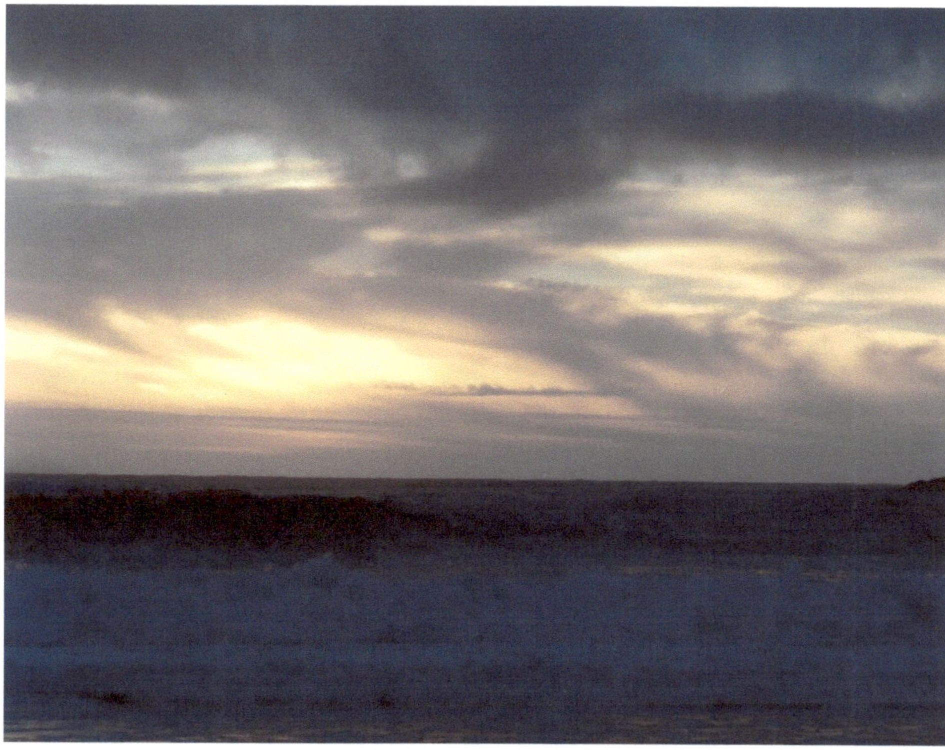

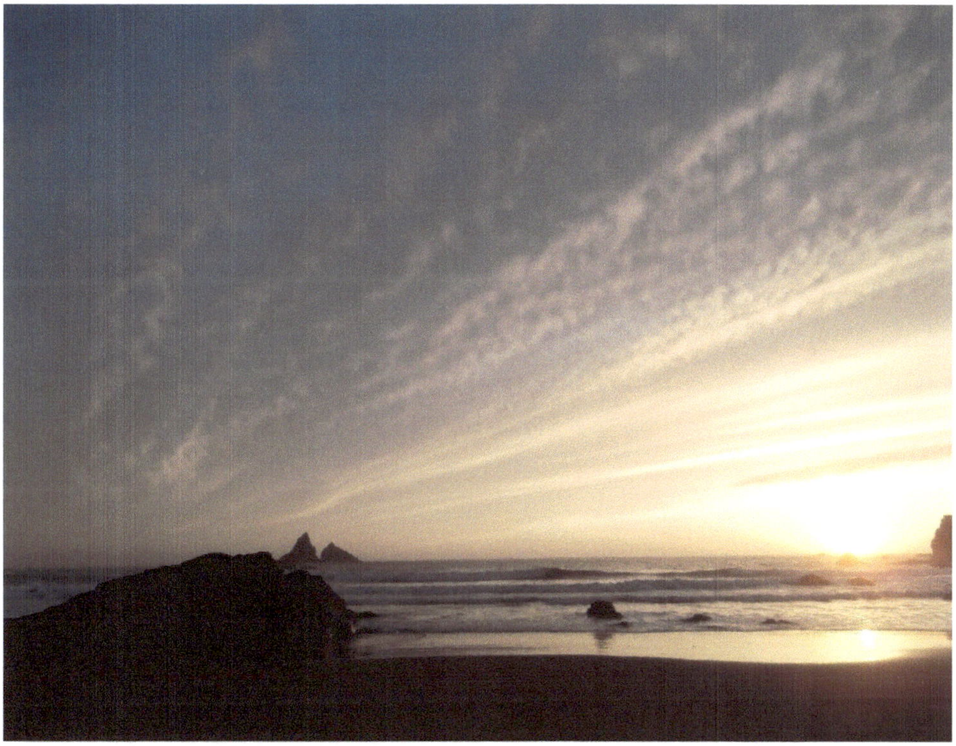

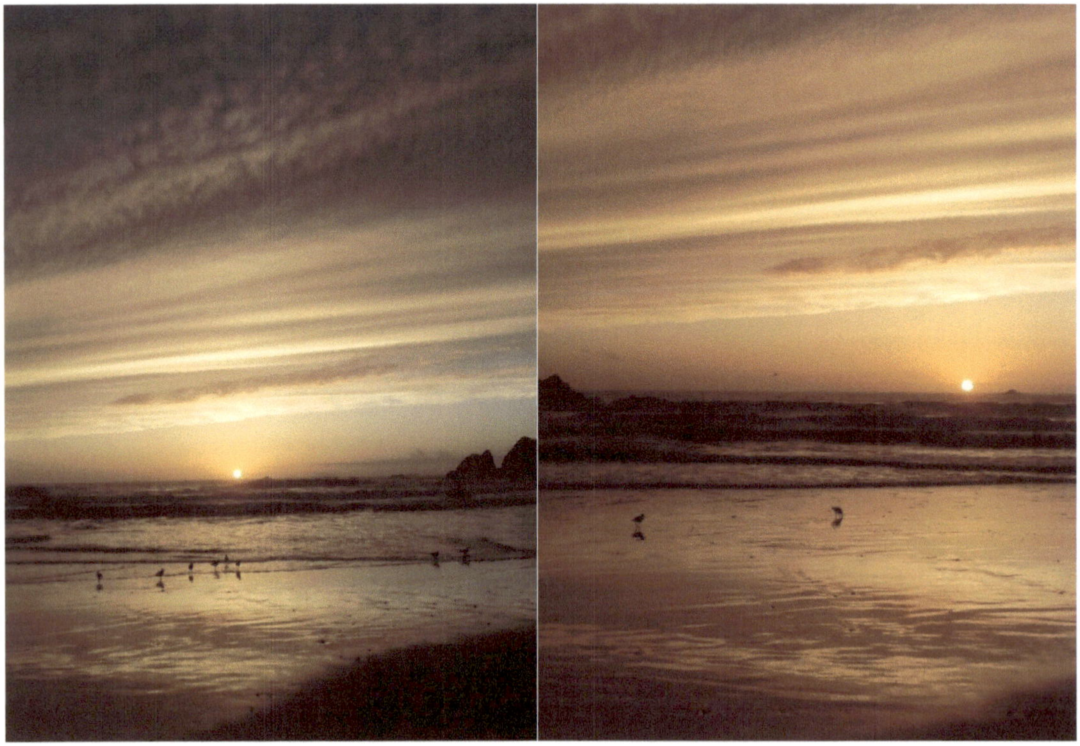

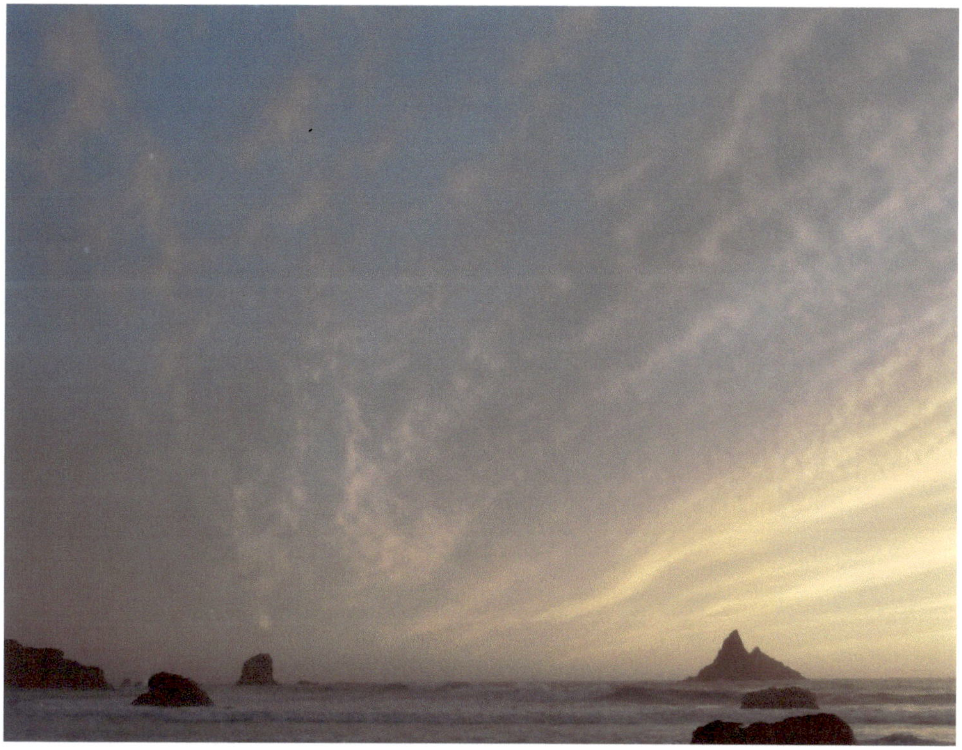

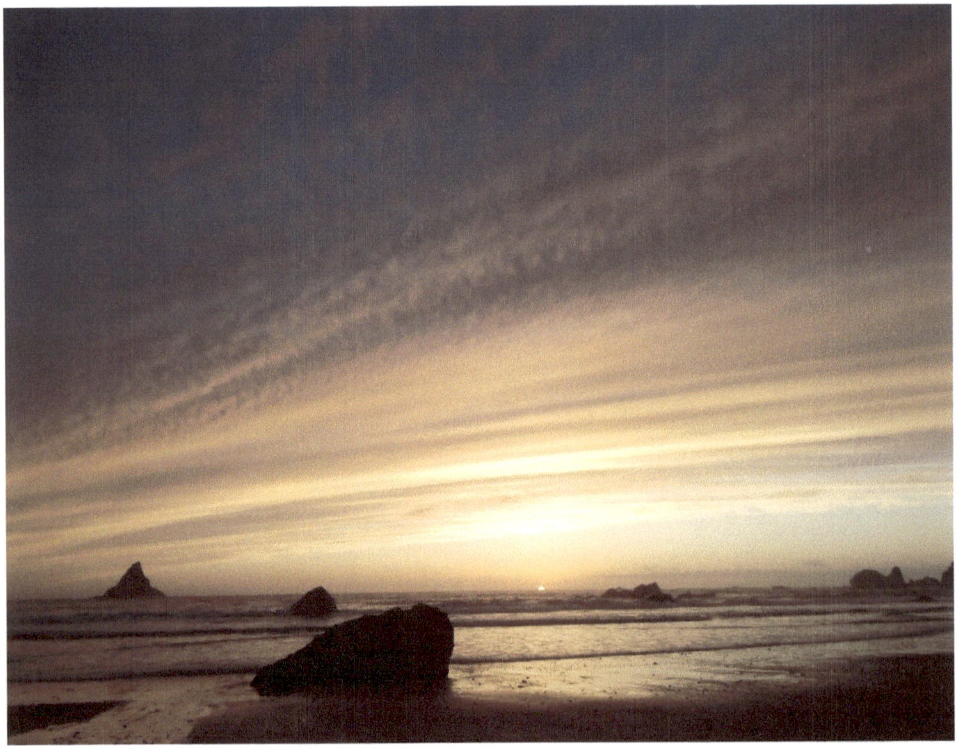

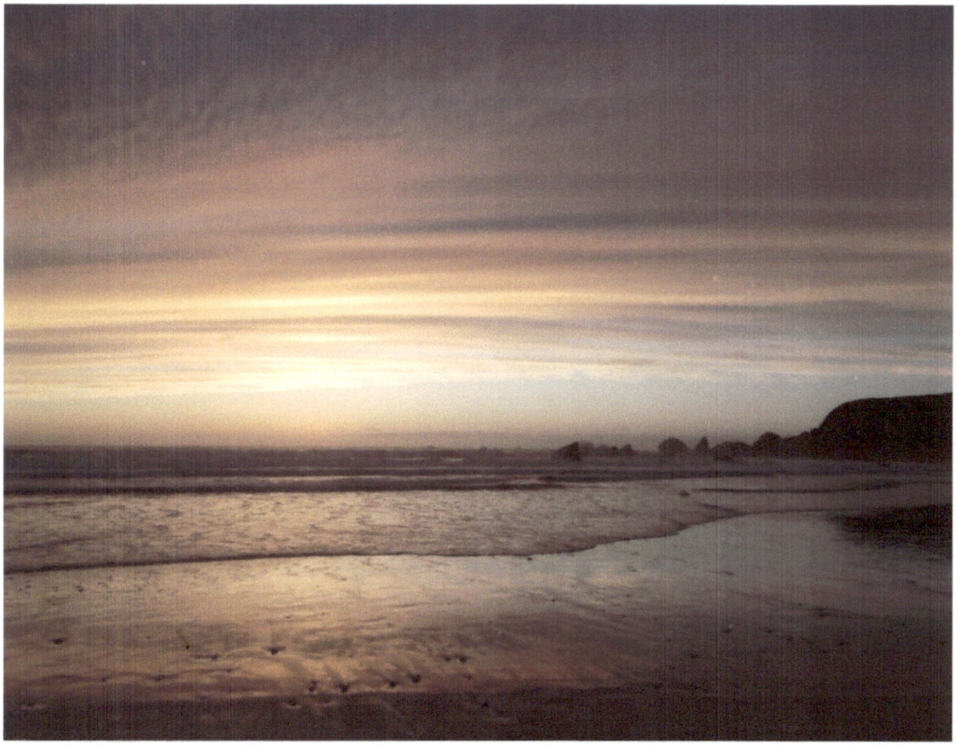

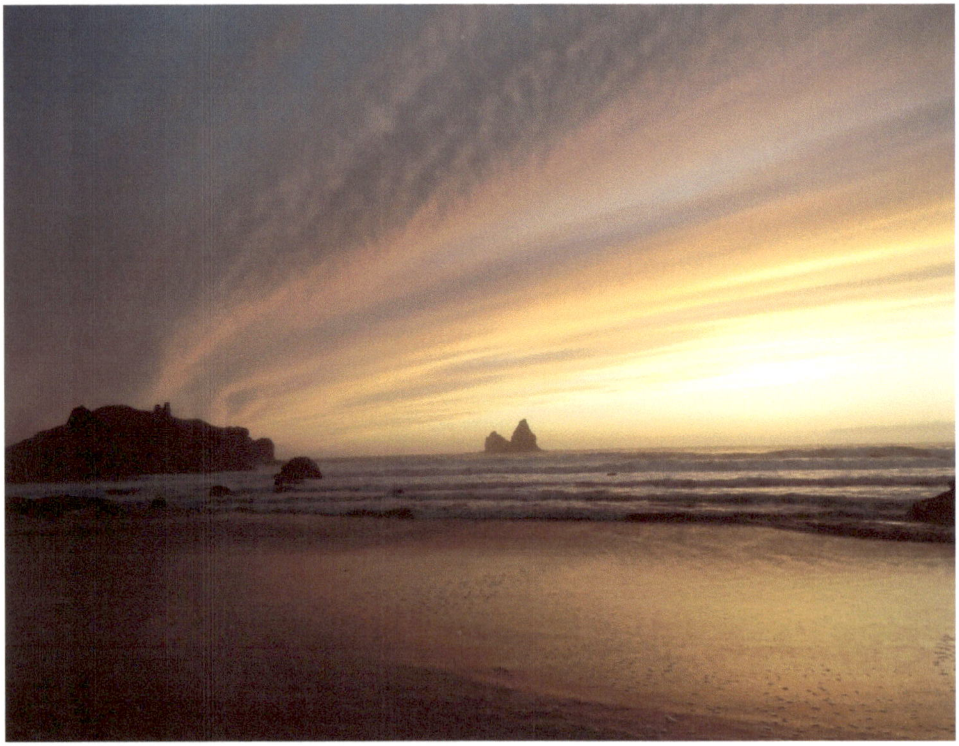

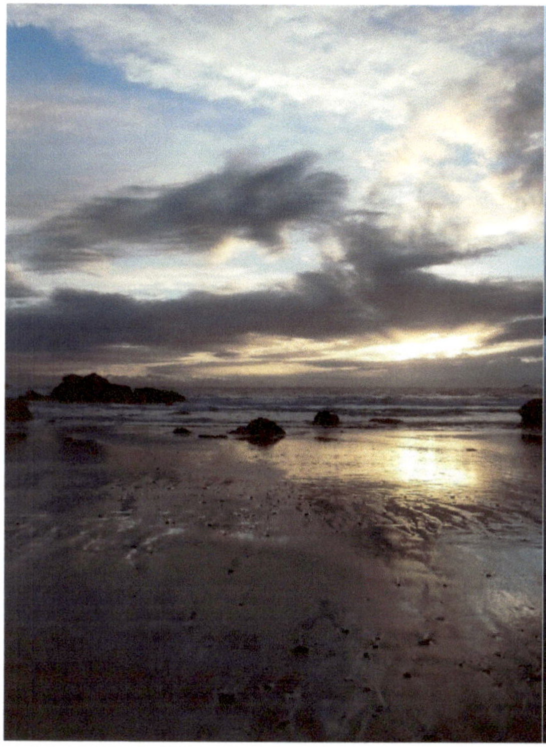
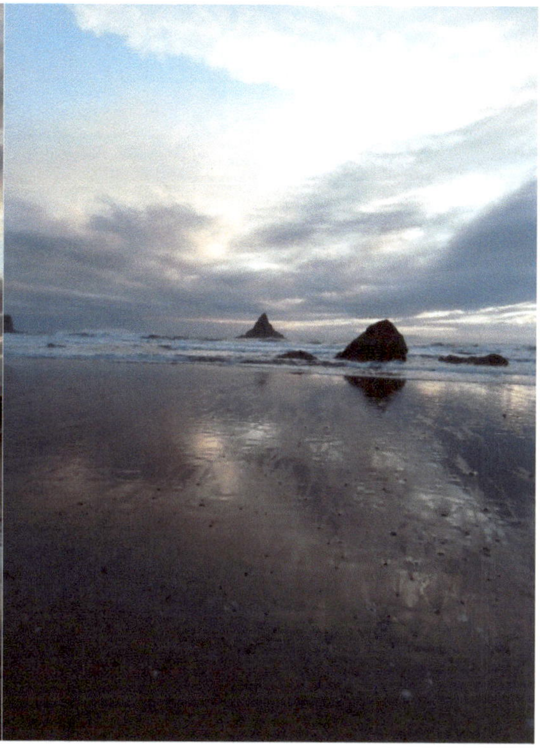

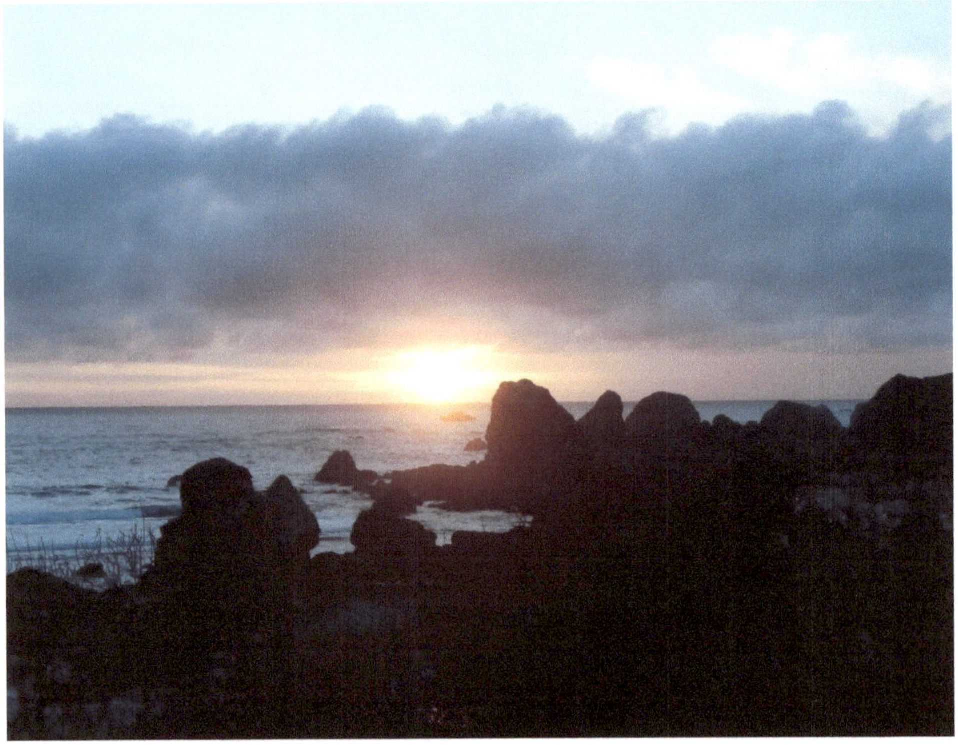

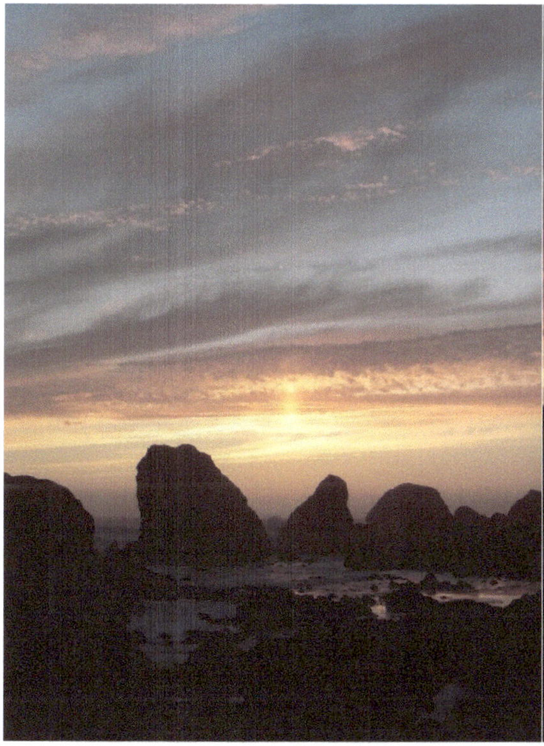
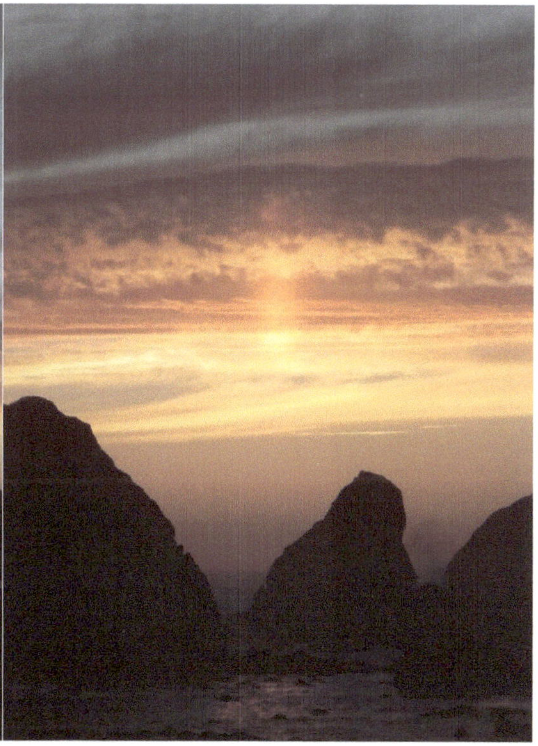

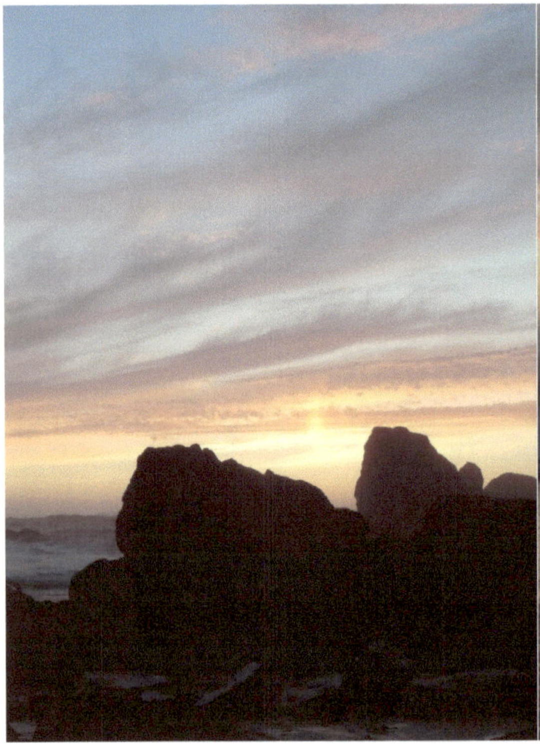
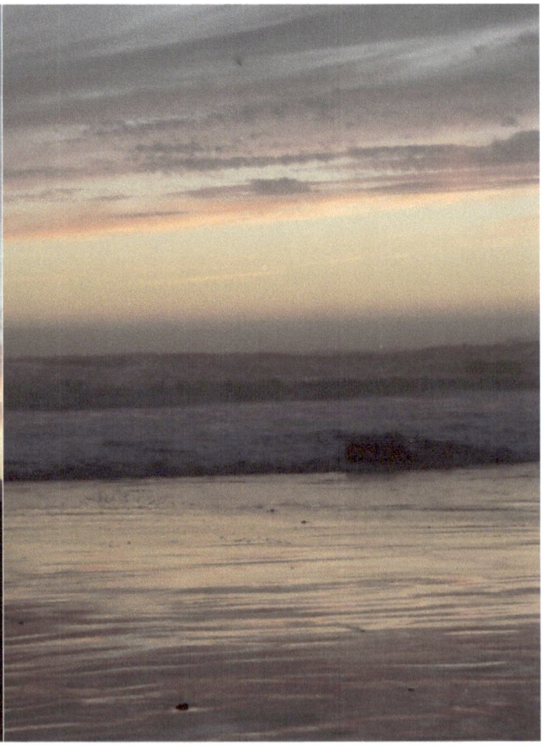

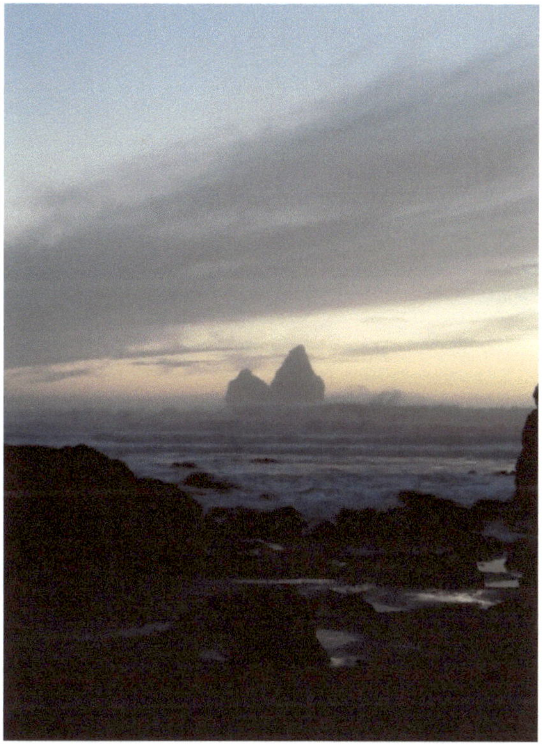

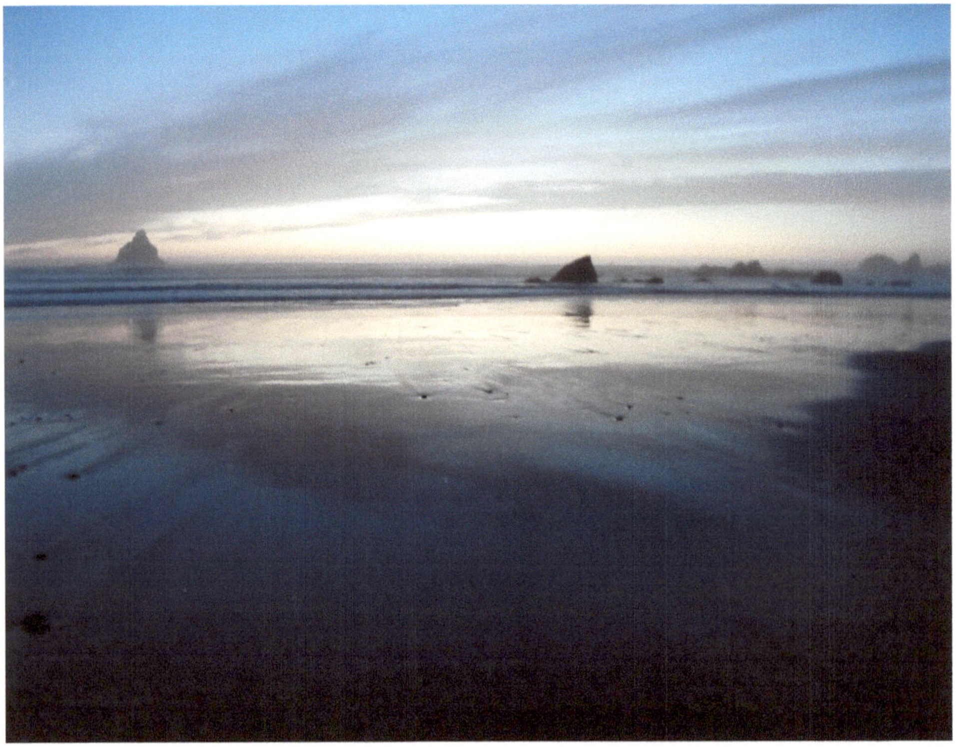

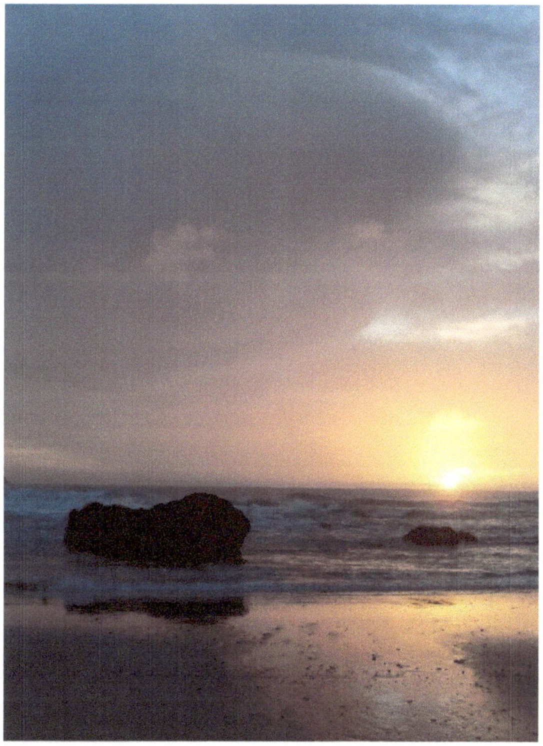

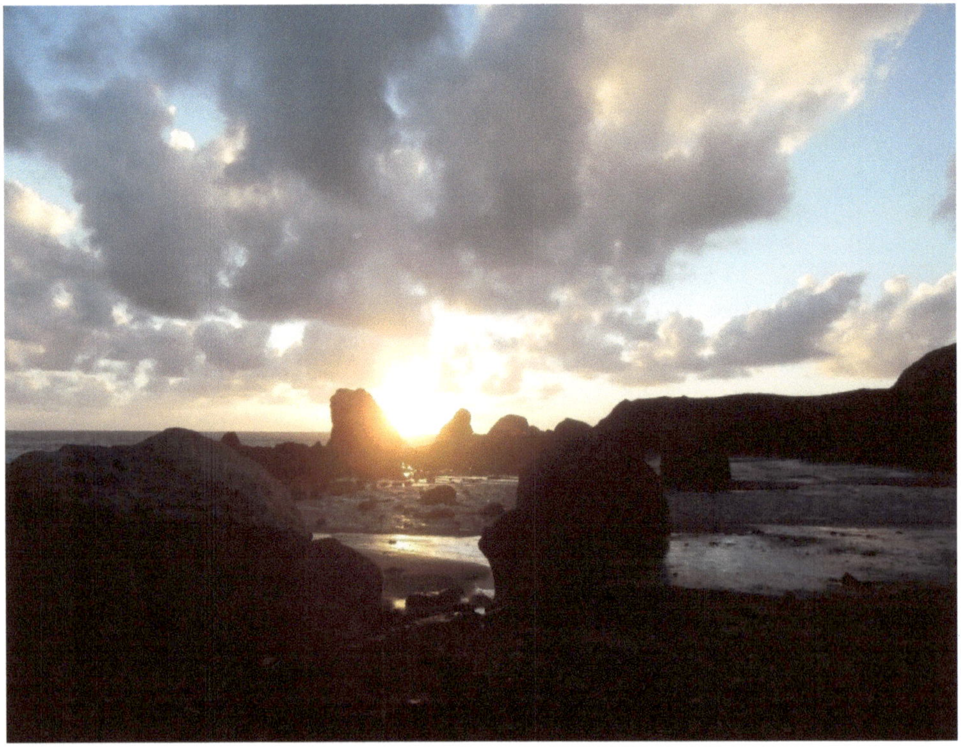

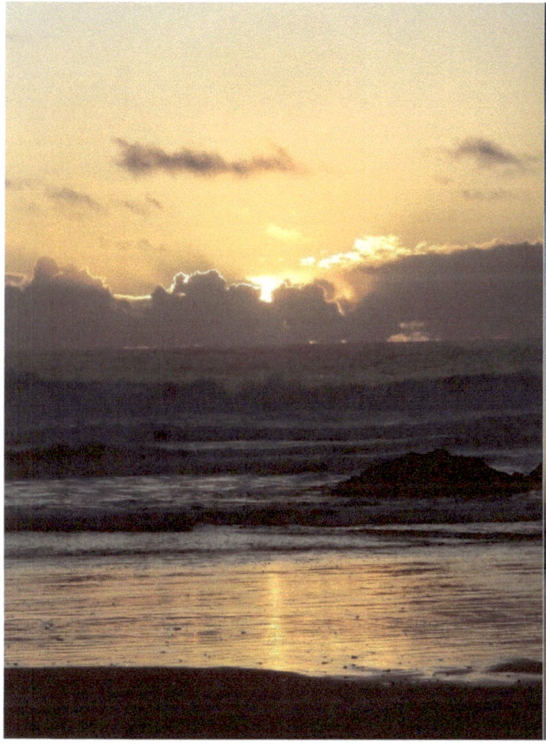
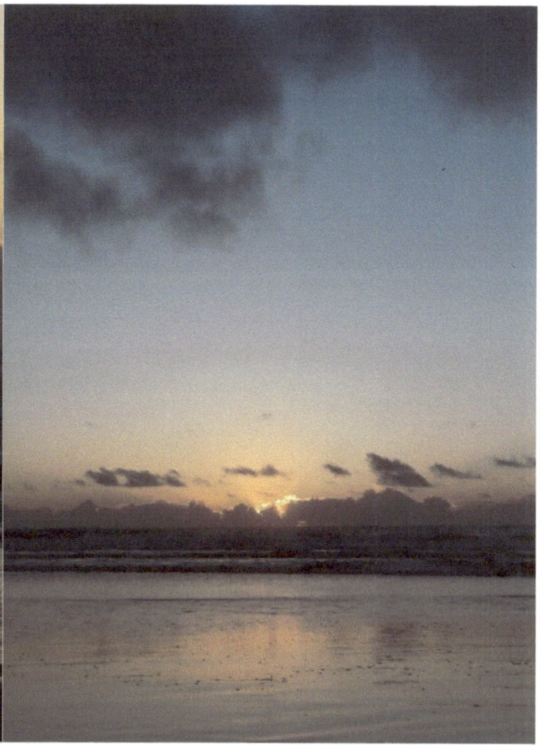

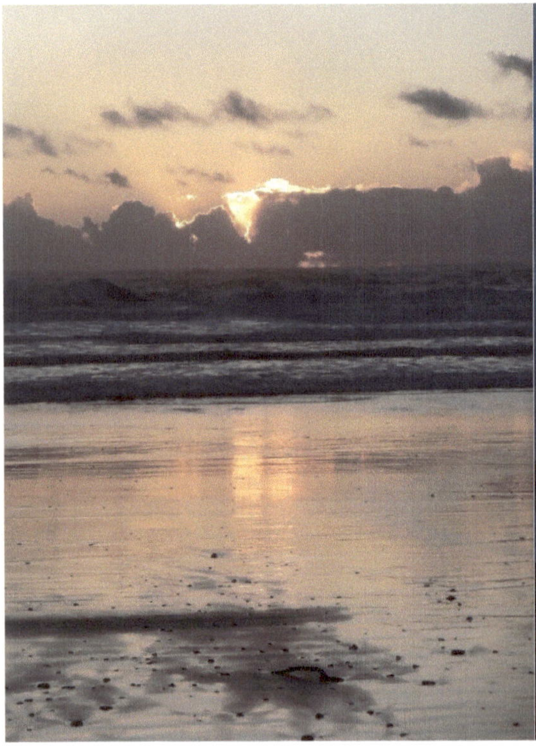
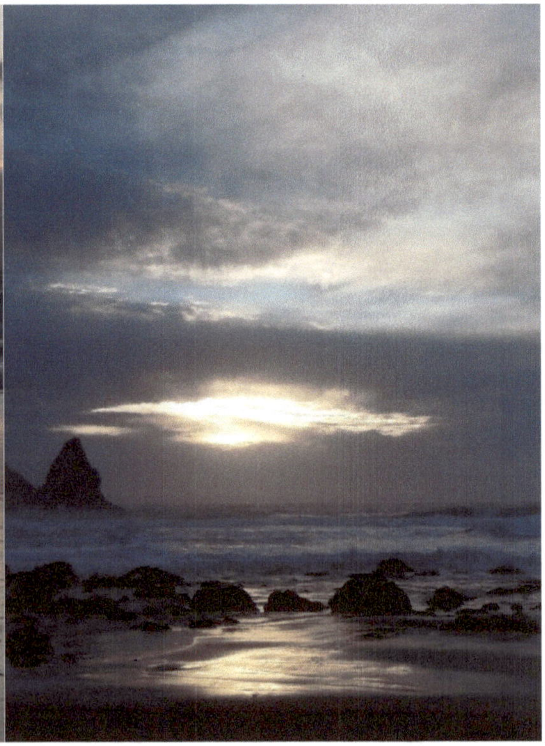

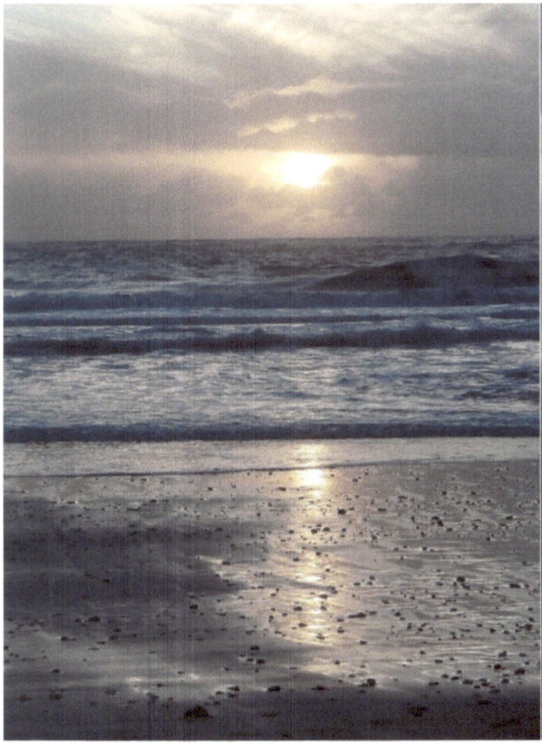

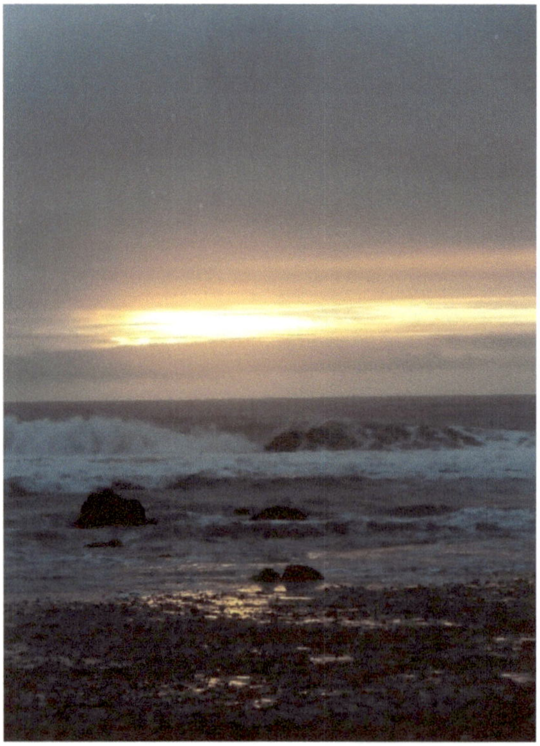

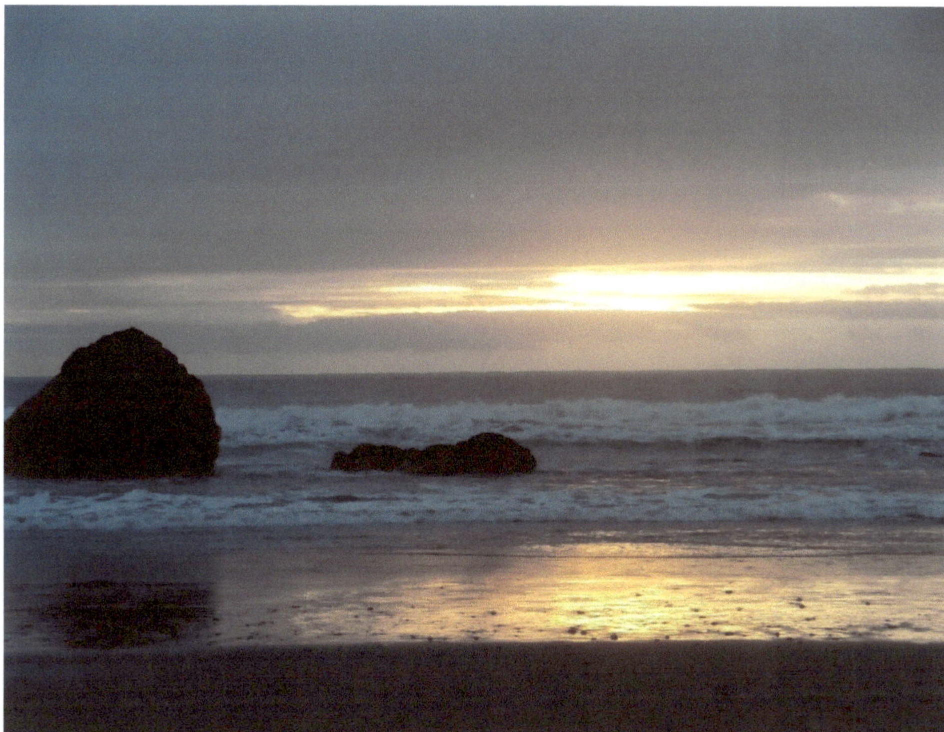

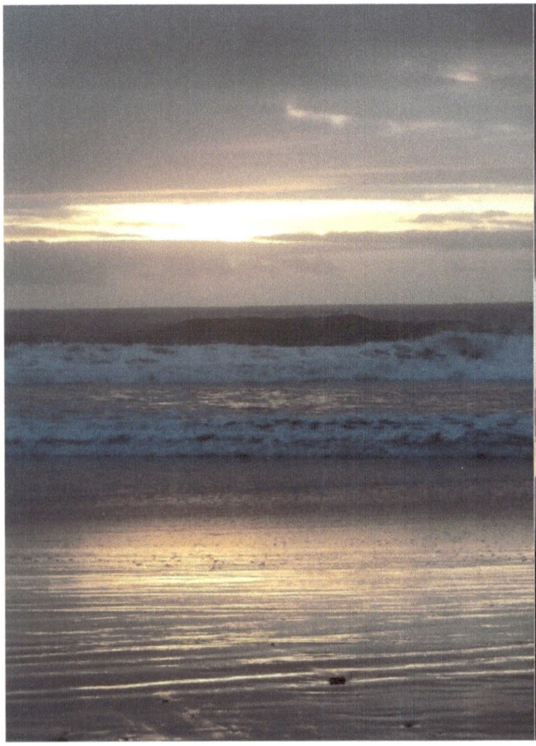
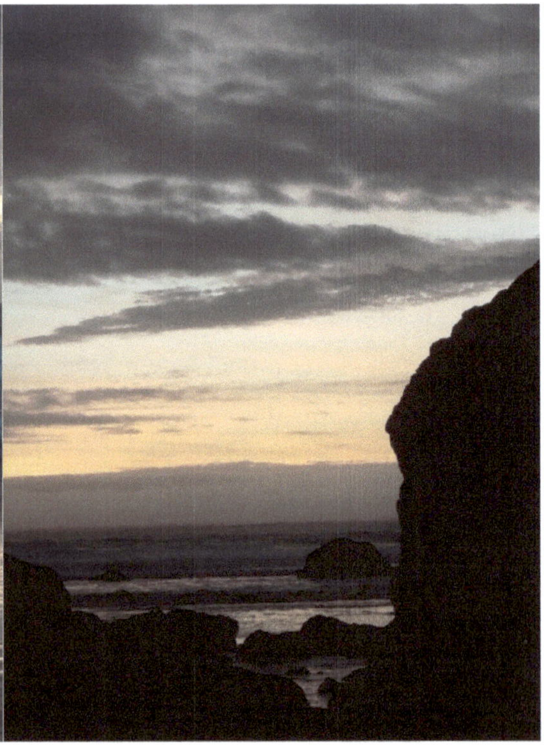

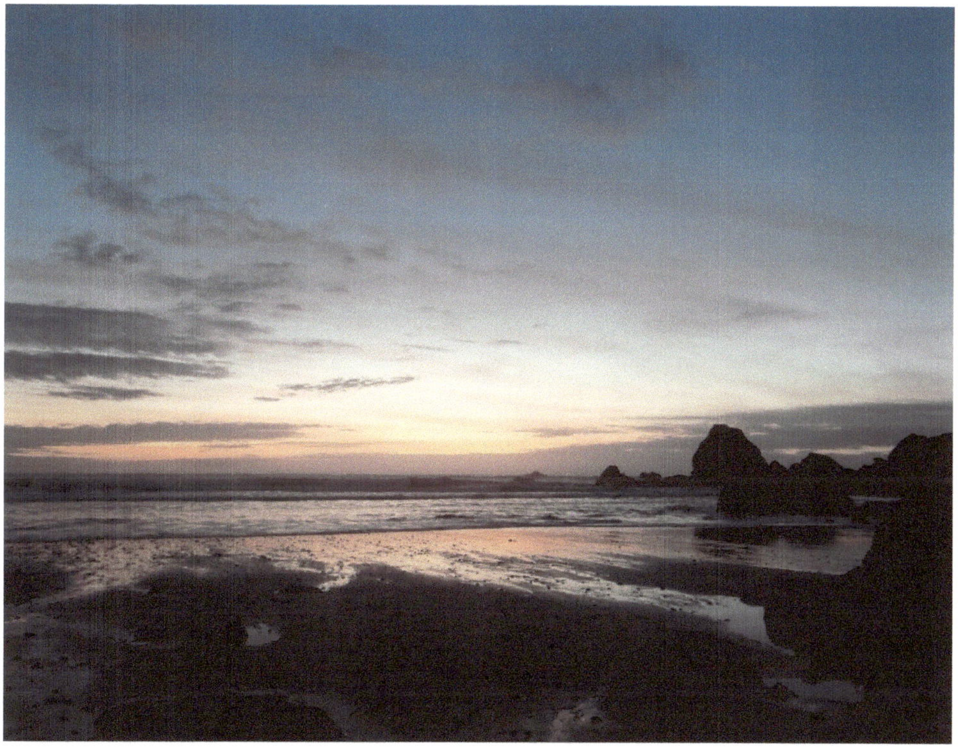

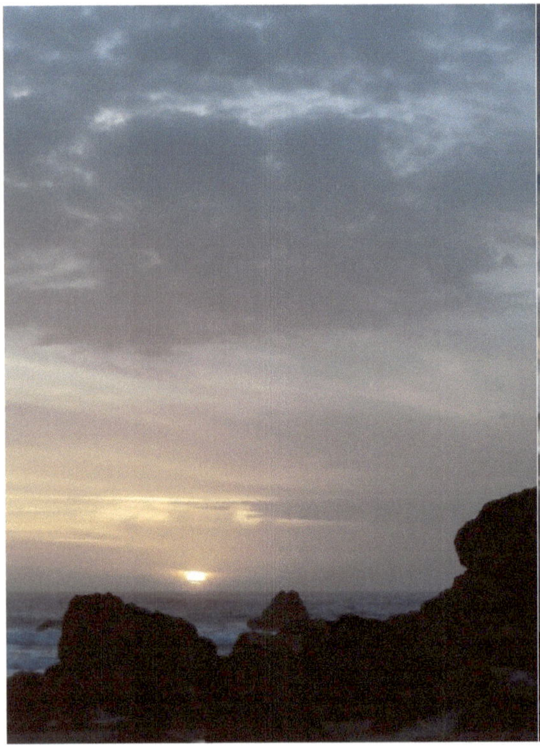
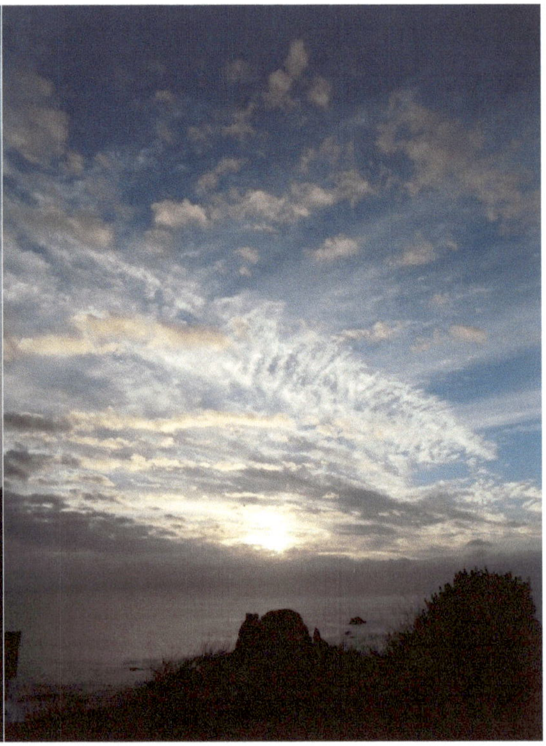

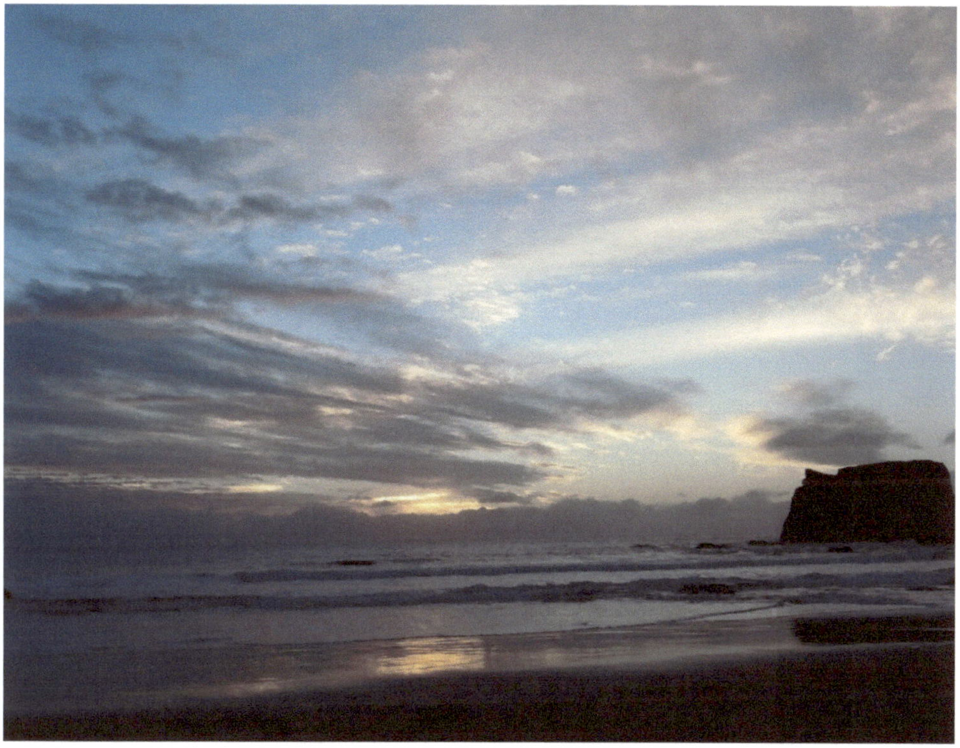

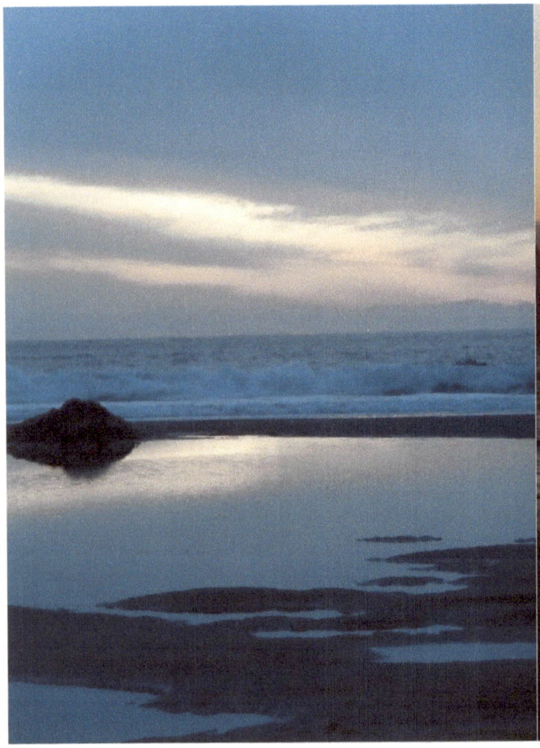
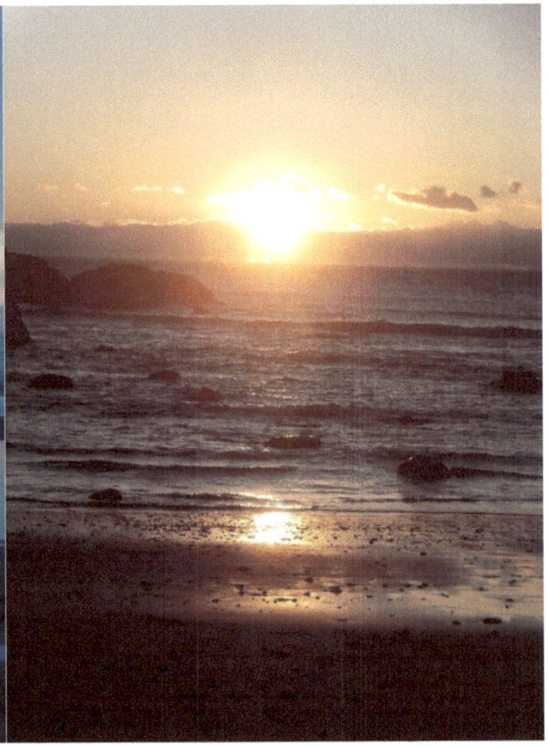

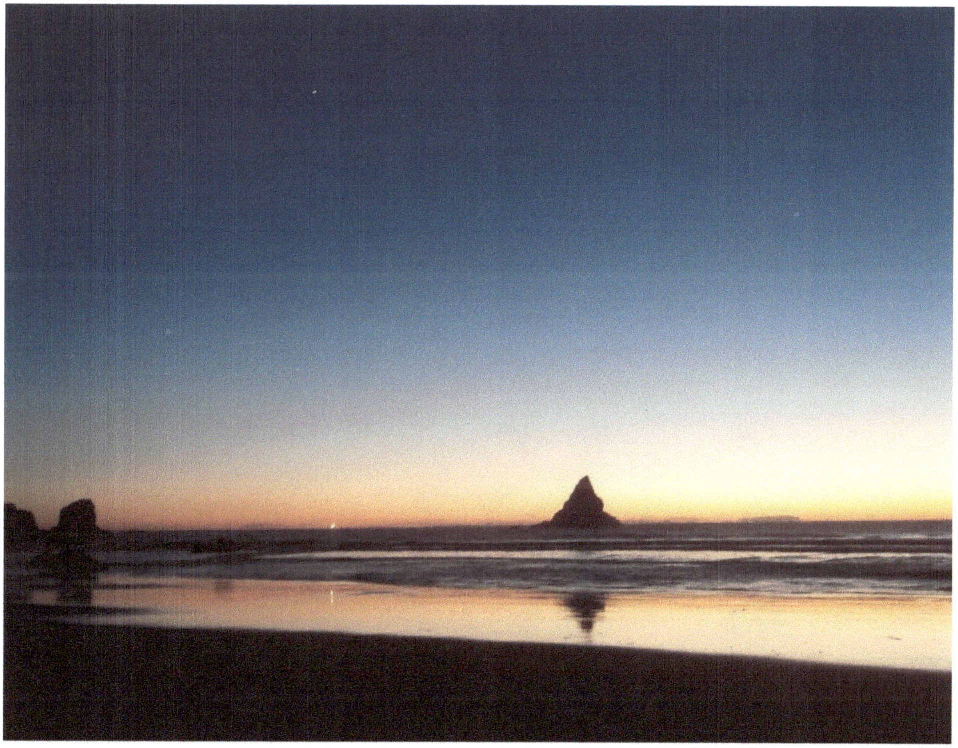

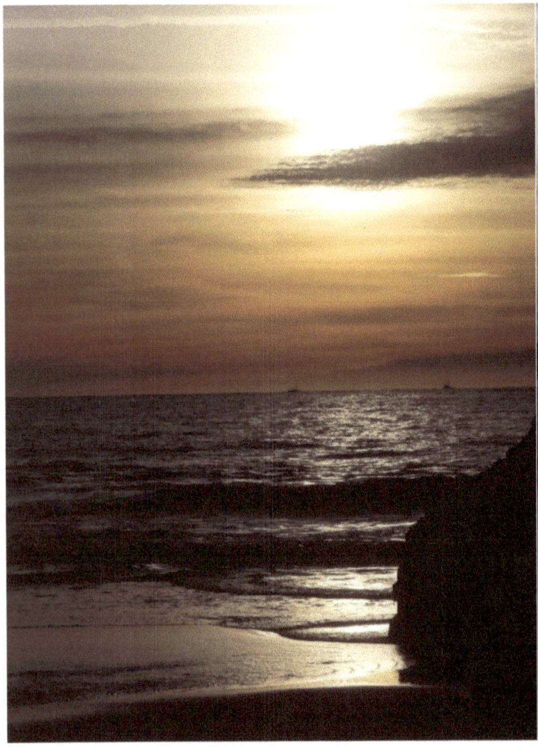
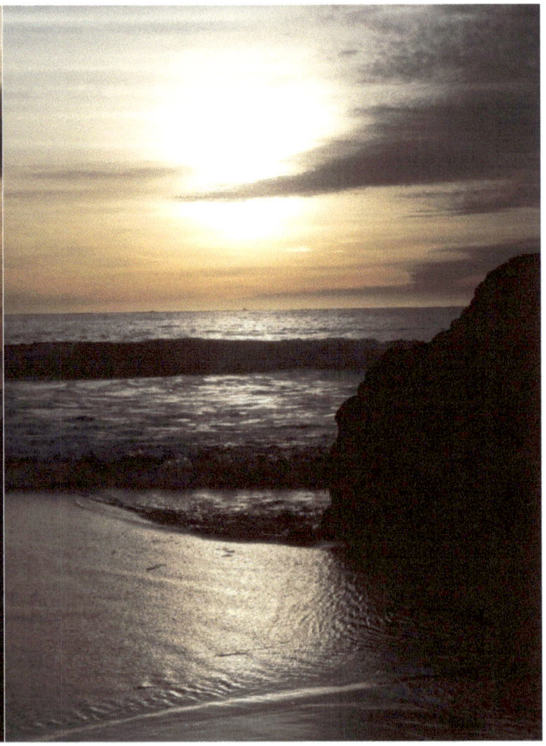

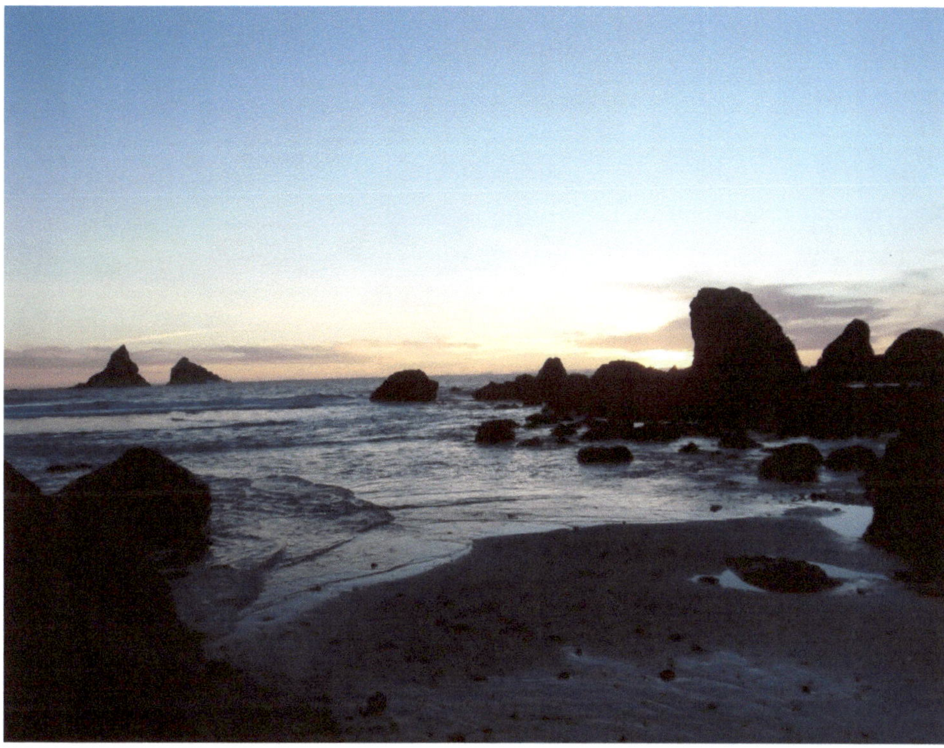

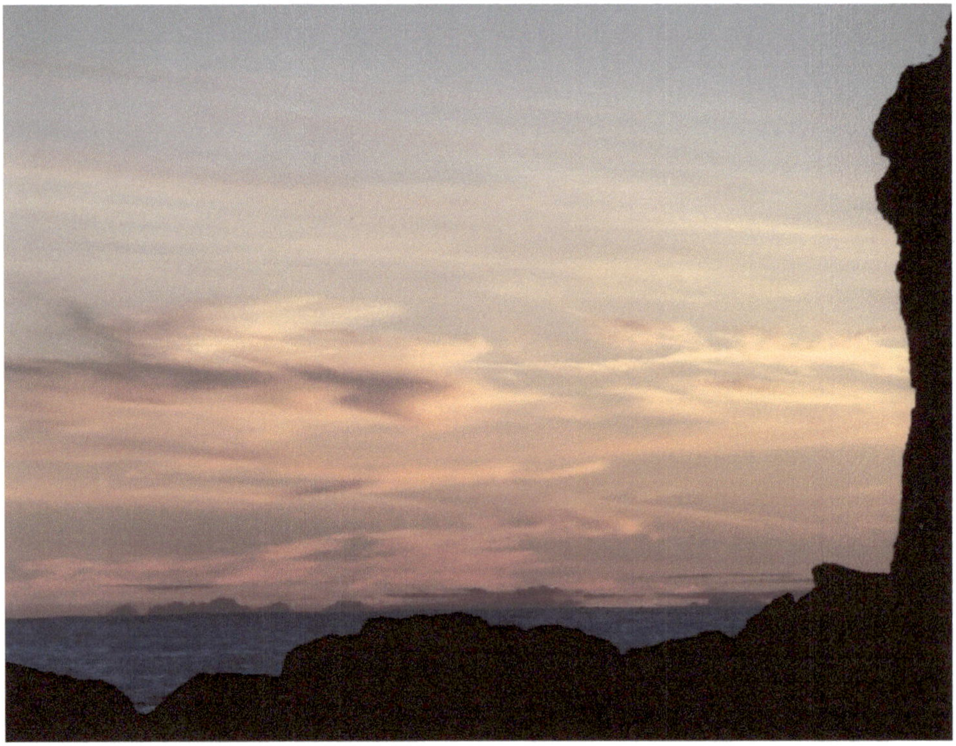

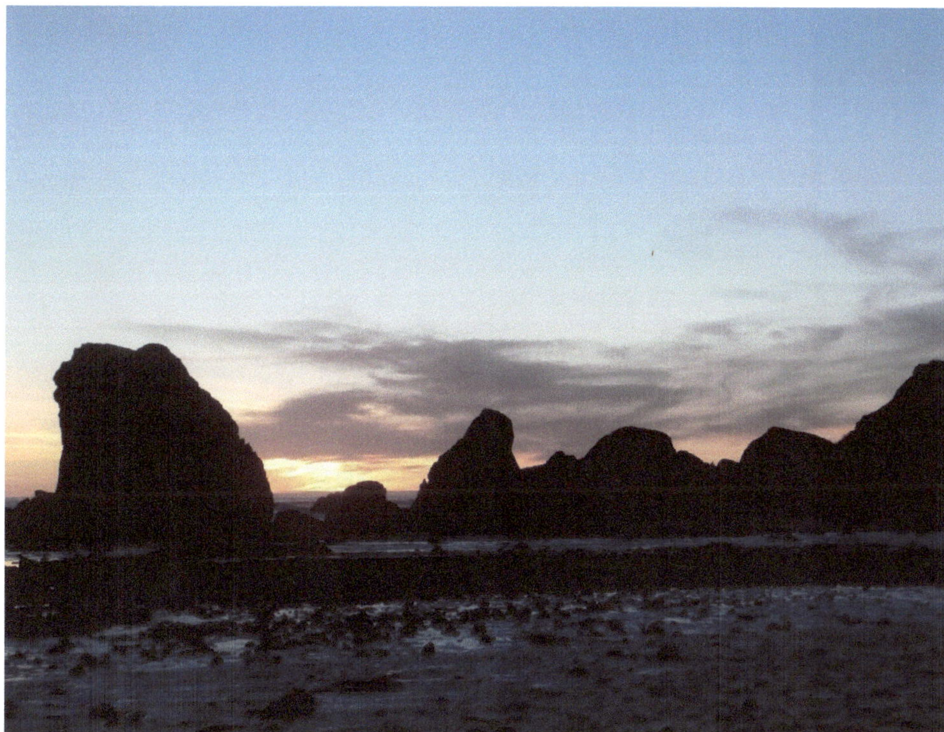

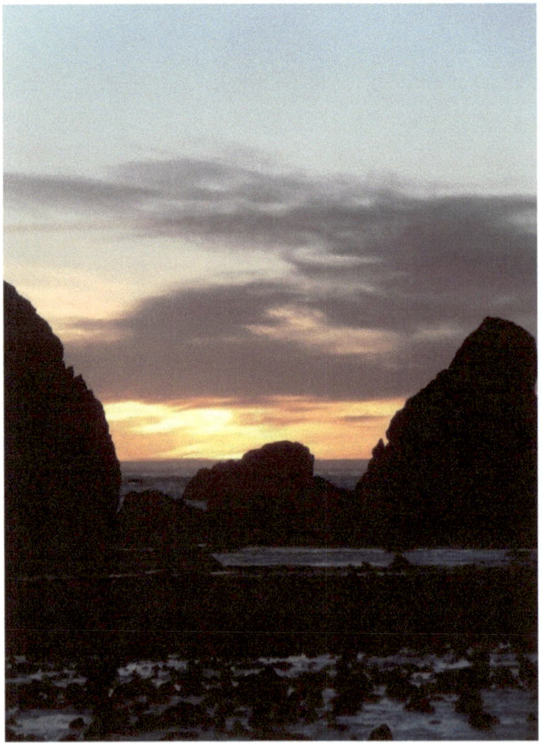

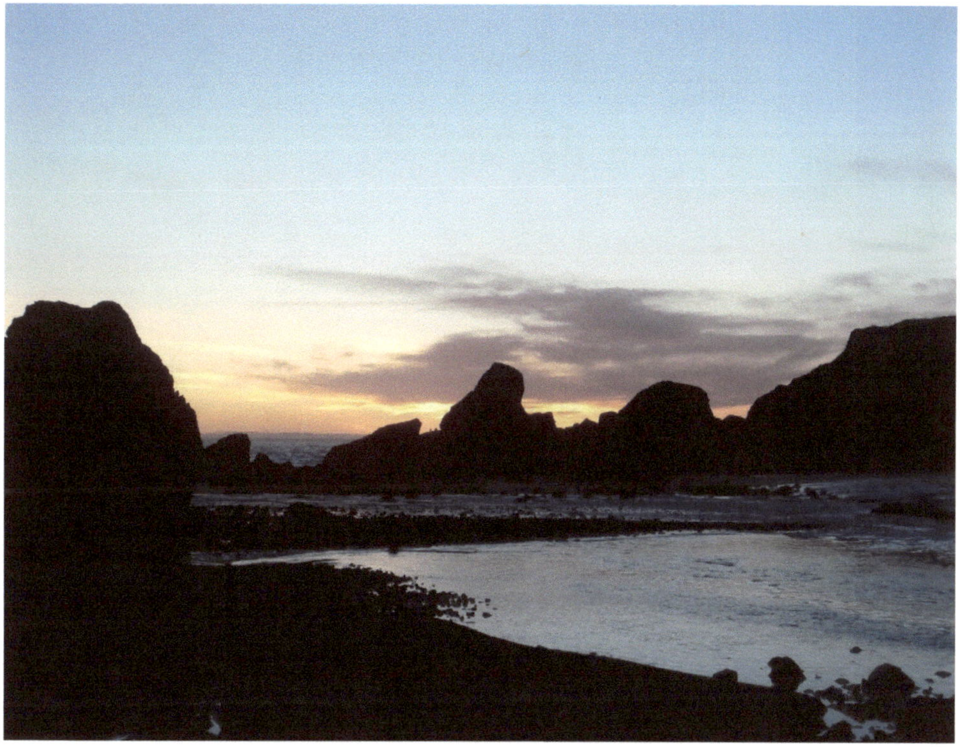

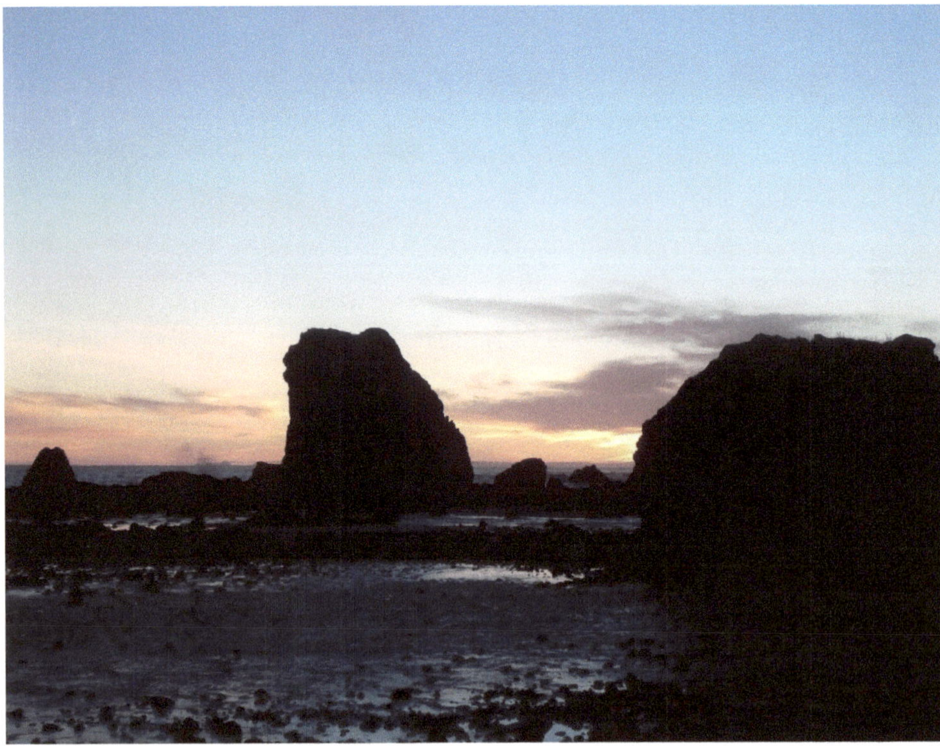

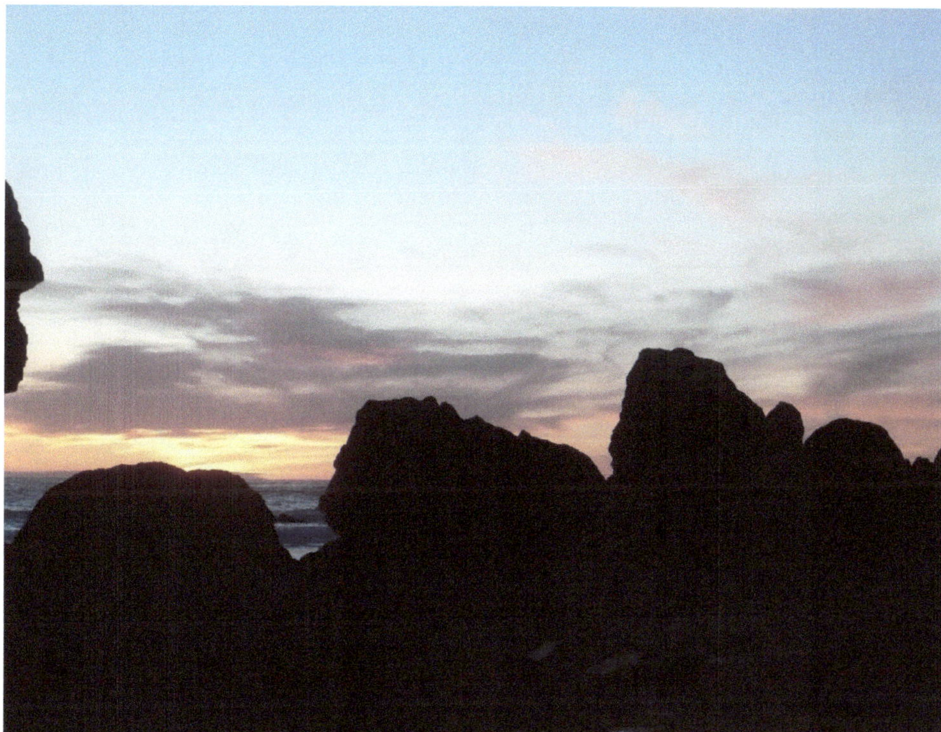

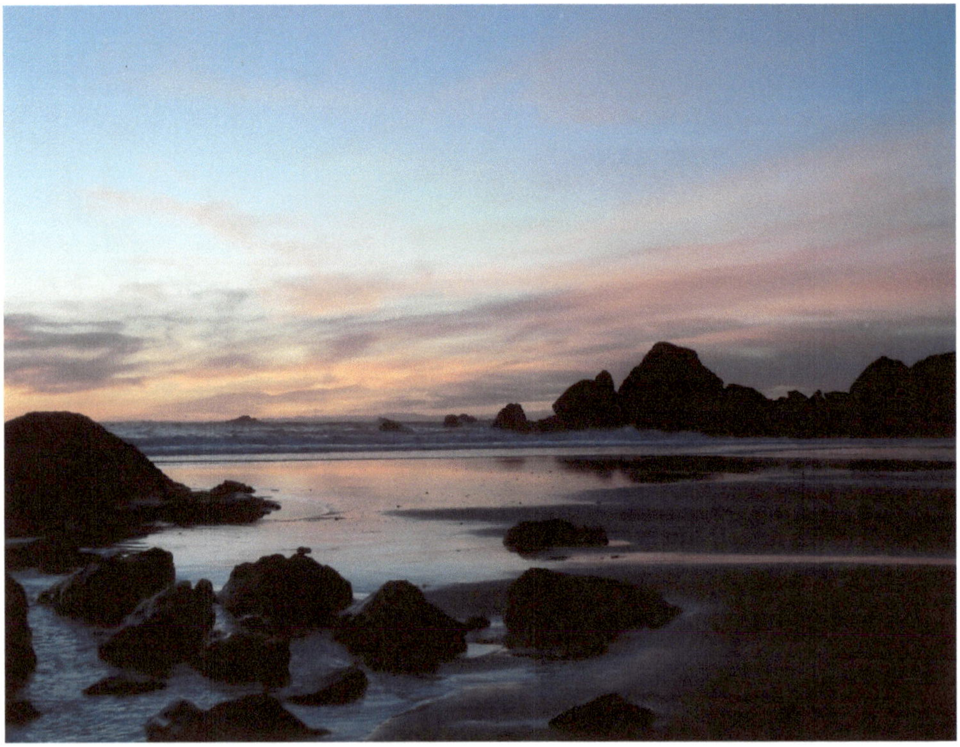

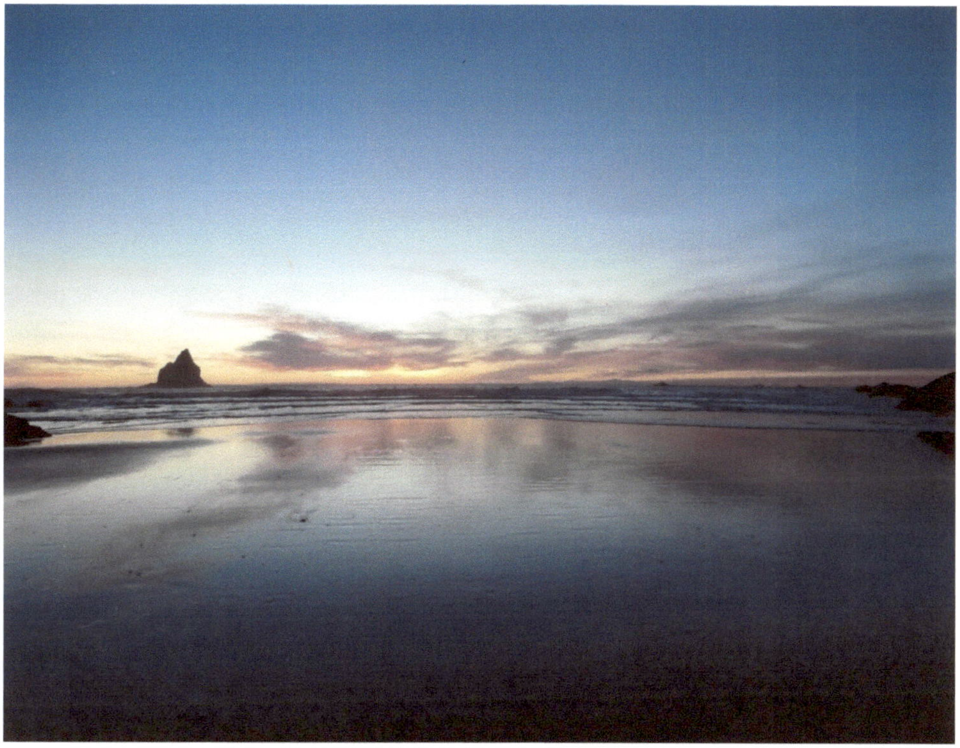

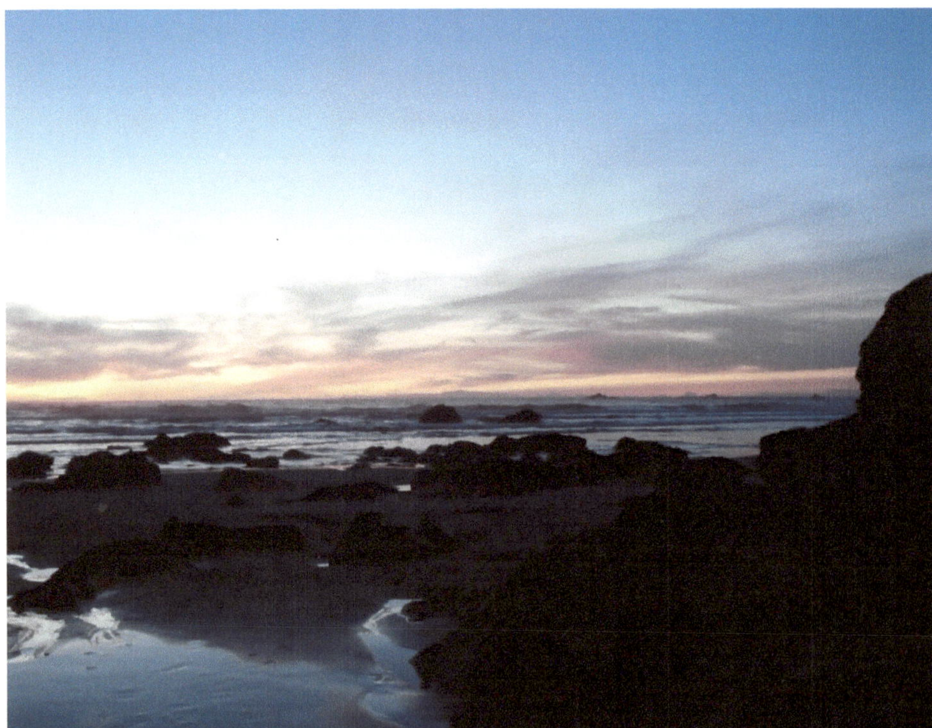

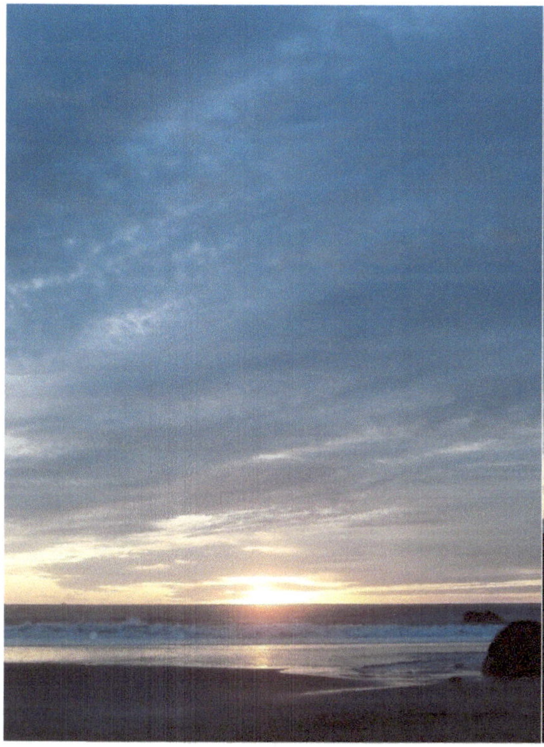
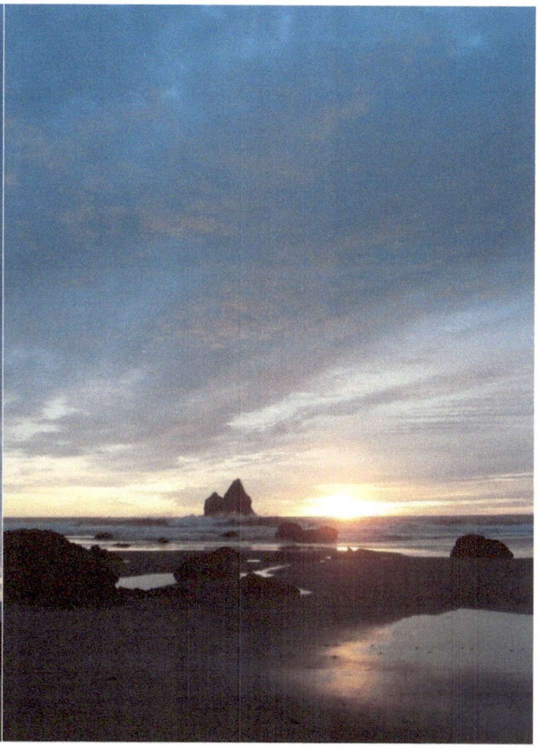

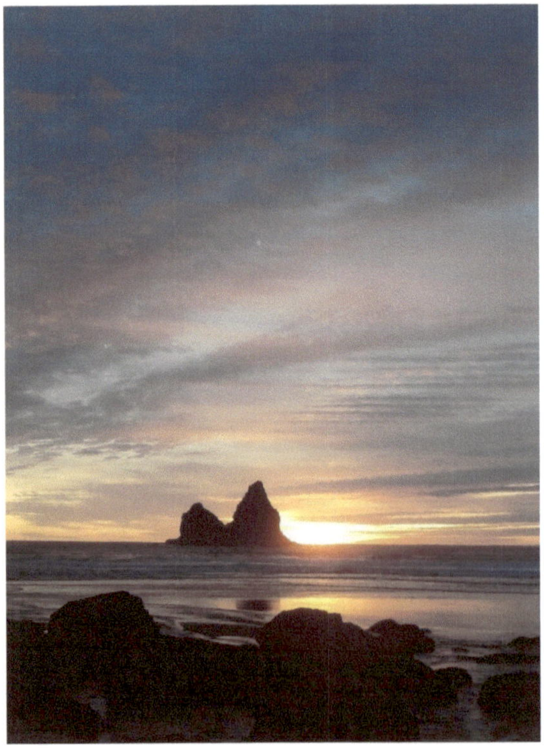

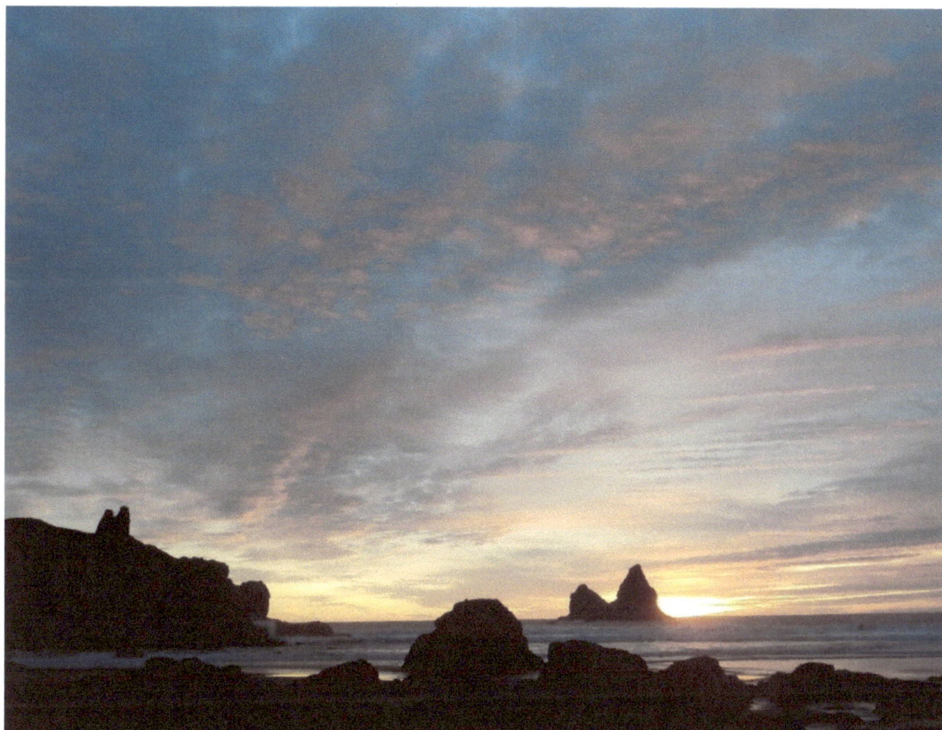

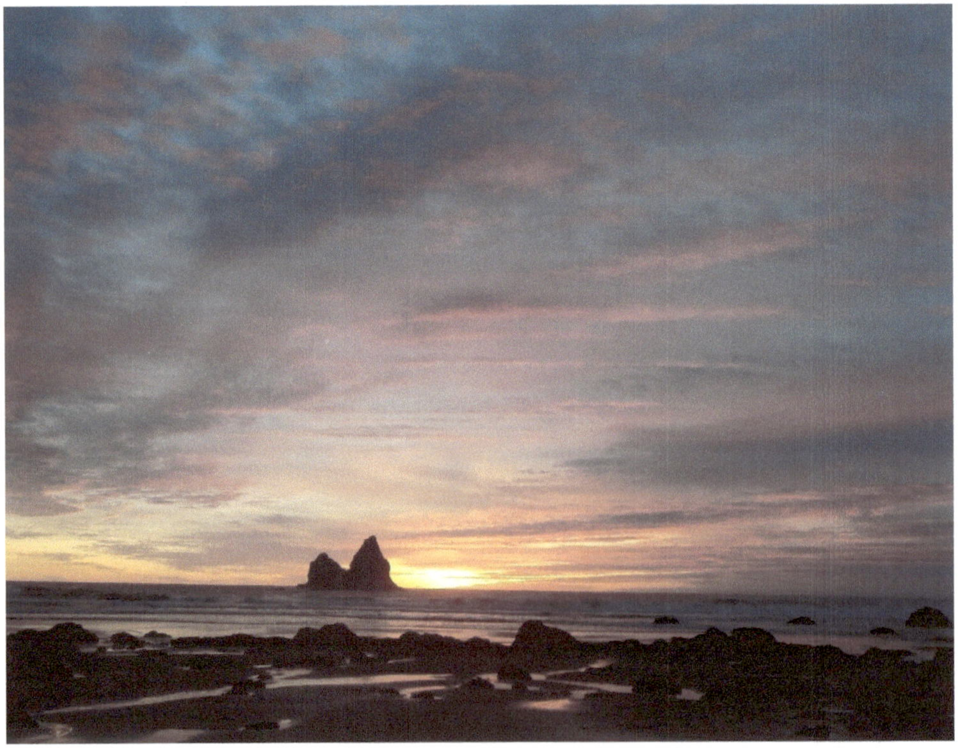

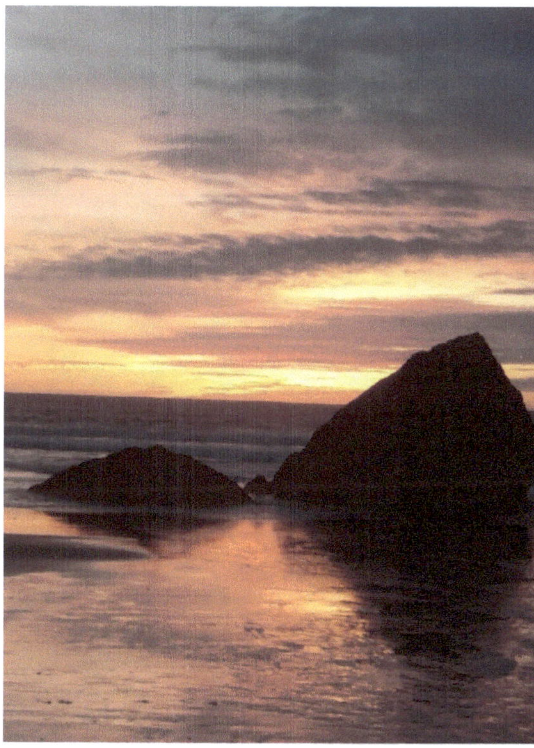
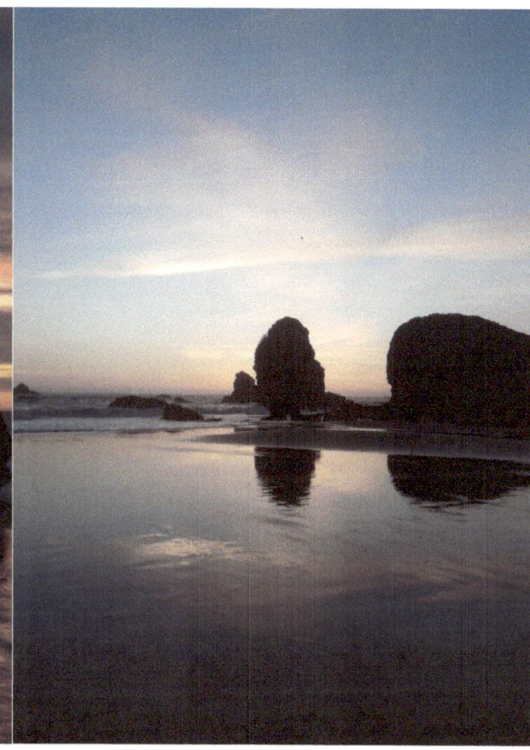

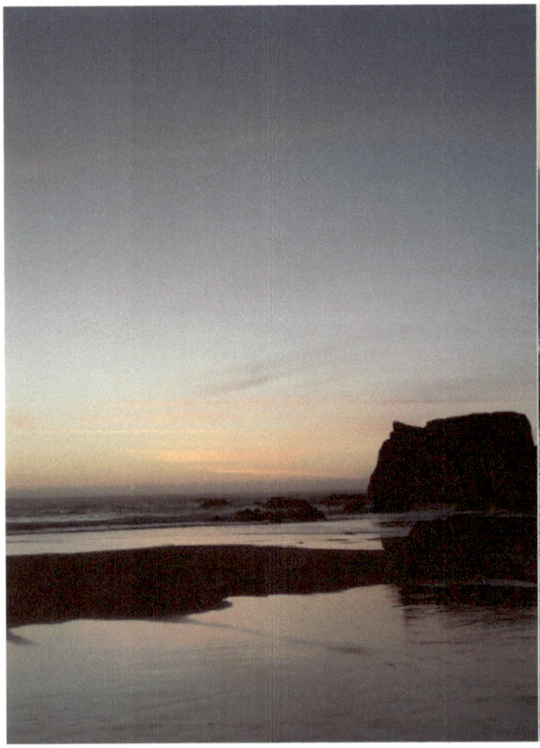
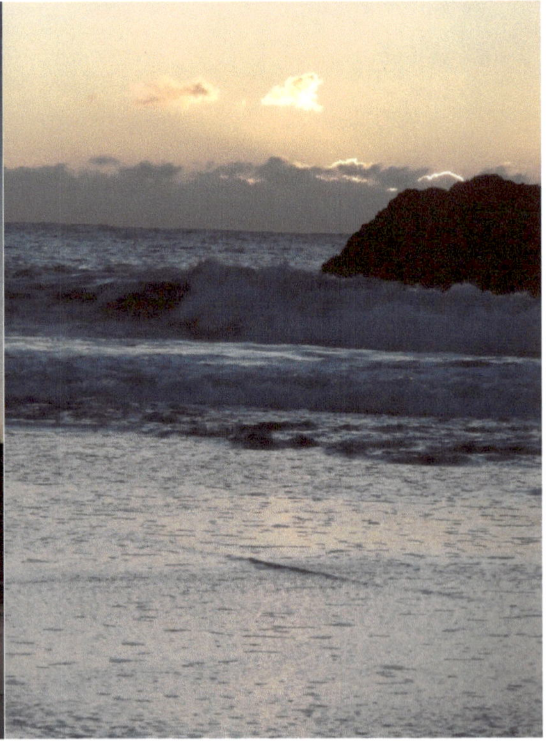

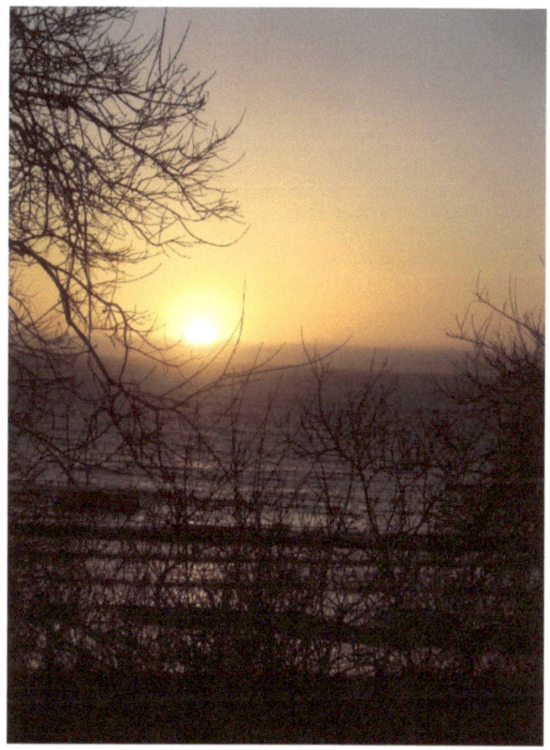

www.ingramcontent.com/pod-product-compliance
Lightning Source LLC
Chambersburg PA
CBHW050806180526
45159CB00004B/1573
* 9 7 8 1 5 4 2 3 8 9 2 8 0 *